Starting Skills in English

Listening and Speaking

Part A

Book Map

Listening (Lessons 1 and 3)	Speaking (Lessons 2 and 4)
Starter	
• target words in isolation • target words in context • predicting next word • hearing /e/, /ɪ/ and /aɪ/ • instructions for classwork • recognizing target questions	• target words in isolation • target words in context • asking target questions • saying /e/, /ɪ/ and /aɪ/ • introducing self (1): age, name, nationality, hometown
Listening (Lessons 1 and 2)	**Speaking (Lessons 3 and 4)**
Theme 1 – Work and Business	
• target words in isolation • target words in context • hearing /ɑː/ and /eɪ/ • identifying key factual information	• target words in isolation • target words in context • saying /ɑː/ and /eɪ/ • asking target questions • introducing self (2): job, date of birth
Theme 2 – Science and Nature	
• target words in isolation • target words in context • hearing /iː/ • understanding descriptions (1)	• target words in isolation • target words in context • saying *can* and *can't* • asking about abilities • asking target questions • describing objects
Theme 3 – The Physical World	
• target words in isolation • target words in context • hearing /aʊ/ • understanding descriptions (2)	• target words in isolation • target words in context • saying /aʊ/ • asking target questions • describing places

Starting Skills in English

Listening and Speaking

Part A

Book Map

Listening (Lessons 1 and 2)	Speaking (Lessons 3 and 4)
Theme 4 – Culture and Civilization	
• target words in isolation • target words in context • hearing /æ/	• target words in isolation • target words in context • asking about new words • the letter *a* • stress within words
Theme 5 – They Made Our World	
• target words in isolation • target words in context • predicting information • hearing /əʊ/	• target words in isolation • target words in context • defining things • saying /əʊ/ and /aʊ/
Theme 6 – Art and Literature	
• target words in isolation • target words in context • preparing to listen: the introduction • guessing information • hearing /ə/ at the end of words	• target words in isolation • target words in context • saying /ə/ at the end of words • talking about the past
Theme 7 – Sports and Leisure	
• target words in isolation • target words in context • predicting the next word or phrase • hearing /ɒ/ and /ɔː/	• target words in isolation • target words in context • talking about figures: bar charts • saying /ɒ/ and /ɔː/
Theme 8 – Nutrition and Health	
• target words in isolation • target words in context • listening for examples • hearing /uː/ and /ʊ/	• target words in isolation • target words in context • doing research: preparing to ask questions • saying /uː/ and /ʊ/

6840402906 1 993

Starting Skills in English ... ng

Garnet EDUCATION

Starting Skills in English

Listening and Speaking

Part A

Contents

Introduction

THIS COURSE IS THE LISTENING AND SPEAKING COMPONENT of Part A of the *Starting Skills in English* series. There are linked components – *Reading and Writing* and *Vocabulary and Grammar.*

The series takes students from False Beginner to Elementary level in the four skills, Listening, Speaking, Reading and Writing. It also ensures that students can use a range of relevant vocabulary and form basic S V(O)(C)(A) sentences.

The Listening and Speaking component is designed to build skills that help students understand and produce short talks in English on a range of topics. It is ideal for students who will go on to study an English for Academic Purposes course.

The course begins with a Starter section which covers the most basic points of English language.

The main part of the course is organized into themes, e.g., *Science and Nature, Art and Literature.* The same themes are used across the three books in Part A. If, therefore, you are studying two or more components, the vocabulary and structures that you learn or practise in one component will be useful in another component.

Within each theme, there are four lessons:

Lesson 1: *Listening*
This is a test lesson. You should get most items right in this lesson. If you get anything wrong, the teacher will help you improve.

Lesson 2: *Listening*
This is a revision and practice lesson. You hear short texts and learn new listening skills.

Lesson 3: *Speaking*
This is a test lesson. You should get most items right in this lesson. If you get anything wrong, the teacher will help you improve.

Lesson 4: *Speaking*
This is a revision and practice lesson. You produce sentences and short texts and learn new speaking skills.

Lesson 1: Listening

A Listen and point.

B Listen and do.

C Listen and answer.

D Right or wrong? Listen and check.

Lesson 1: Listening

E Look.

1	2	3	4
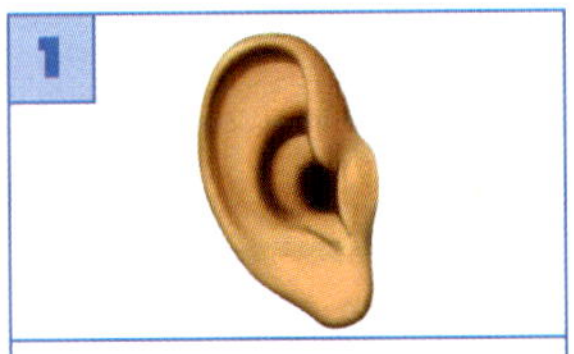	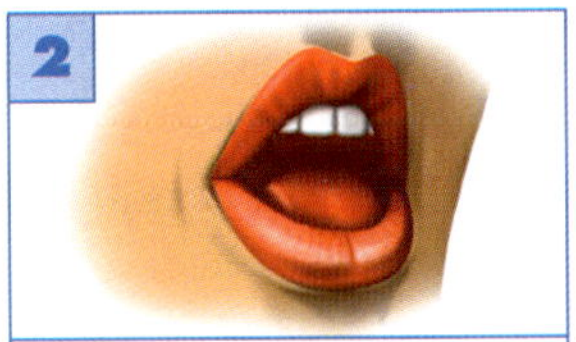	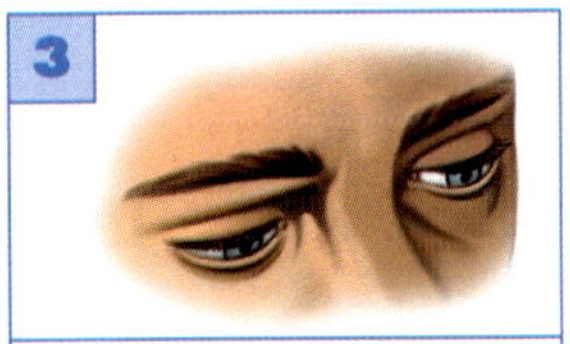	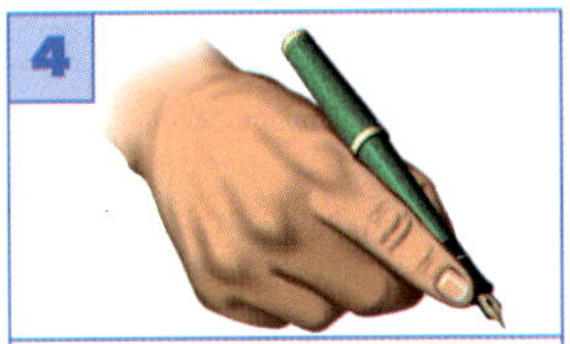
listen	**speak**	**read**	**write**

1 Listen.

2 Listen and do.

3 Listen, read and speak.

F Read.

1 Listen and number.

2 Ask and answer.

student		ask	
begin		question	
answer	1	test	
end			

What's number 1?

Answer.

Yes. That's right.

What's number 2?

End.

No. That's wrong.

Ask.

Yes. That's right.

G Listen and tick (✓) the next word.

10	
board	
book	✓
name	
sentence	

H Listen and tick (✓) the question.

Are you a student?	
Are you English?	
Are you at school?	
What class are you in?	
What's the name of your book?	
What's your name?	✓

Skills Check

Hearing /e/

Listen. Tick (✓) the words with /e/.

desk	✓	sentence	
pen		student	
end		English	
begin		write	
test		listen	
question		answer	

Lesson 2: Speaking

A **Look. Name the people and things.**

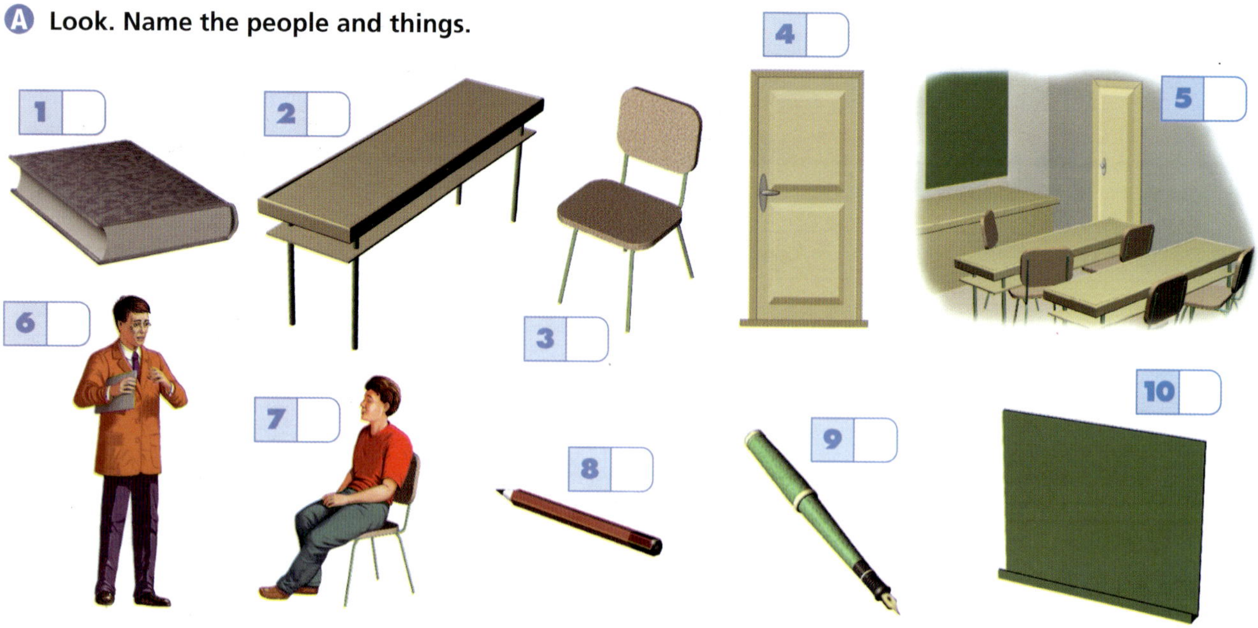

B **Look. Name the actions.**

C **Read and ask.**

name?	
English?	
at school?	
student?	
class?	

D **Right or wrong? Listen and check.**

Lesson 2: Speaking

E **Look at the pictures.**

1 Listen.

2 Listen and answer.

3 Listen and ask.

F **Work in pairs.**

1 Ask and answer.
Student 1: You are Esteban.
Student 2: Ask Esteban questions.

2 Swap roles.

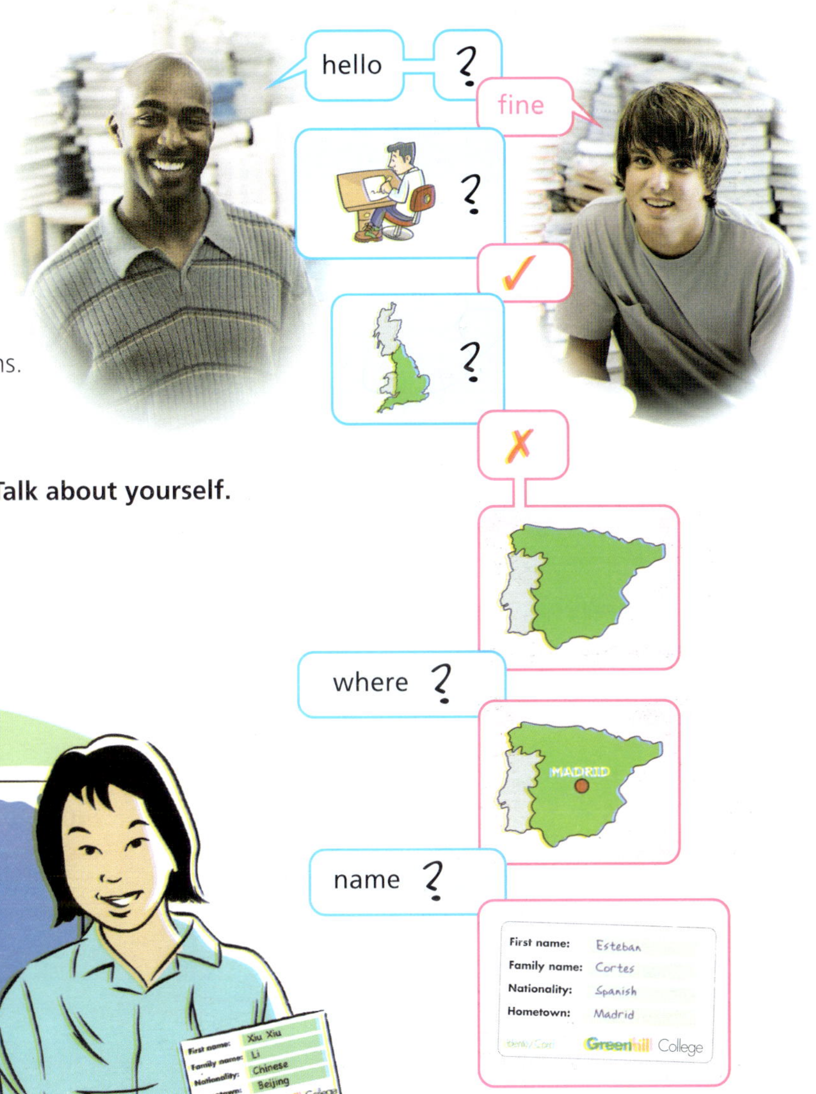

G **Work in pairs. Ask and answer. Talk about yourself.**

H **Look at the picture.**

1 Make sentences.

2 Listen and check.

I **Talk about yourself to the class.**

Skills Check

Saying /e/

Say these words.

hello	question	desk
test	sentence	end
check	pen	yes

Lesson 3: Listening

2006

January	February	March	April	May	June
July	August	September	October	November	December

AUGUST 2006

Monday	Tuesday	Wednesday	Thursday	Friday	Saturday	Sunday
		1	2	3	4	5
6	7	8	9	10	11	12
13	14	15	16	17	18	19
20	21	22	23	24	25	26
27	28	29	30	31		

THURSDAY 31st AUGUST

8.00 a.m.	*Go to college*	3.00 p.m.	
9.00 a.m.	*Lesson 1*	4.00 p.m.	*Lesson 7*
10.00 a.m.		5.00 p.m.	*Go home*
11.00 a.m.	*Lesson 3*	6.00 p.m.	
12.00 p.m.	*Lunch*	7.00 p.m.	
1.00 p.m.		8.00 p.m.	
2.00 p.m.	*Lesson 5*	9.00 p.m.	

A Listen and point.

B Listen and write.

C Listen and answer.

D Right or wrong? Listen and check.

Lesson 3: Listening

E **Look.** ⇨

1 Listen.

2 Listen and do.

3 Listen and speak.

Morning	**Afternoon**	**Evening**	**Night**
6.00 a.m.	12.00 p.m.	6.00 p.m.	12.00 a.m.
7.00 a.m.	1.00 p.m.	7.00 p.m.	1.00 a.m.
8.00 a.m.	2.00 p.m.	8.00 p.m.	2.00 a.m.
9.00 a.m.	3.00 p.m.	9.00 p.m.	3.00 a.m.
10.00 a.m.	4.00 p.m.	10.00 p.m.	4.00 a.m.
11.00 a.m.	5.00 p.m.	11.00 p.m.	5.00 a.m.

F **Read.**

1 Listen and number.

2 Ask and answer.

day	
first	
last	
month	1
time	
week	
year	
today	
now	

Skills Check

Hearing /ɪ/ and /aɪ/

Listen. Tick (✓) the correct column.

	/ɪ/ (it)	/aɪ/ (I)
is	✓	
I'm		✓
begin		
English		
fifteen		
find		
fine		
five		
listen		
my		
night		
tick		
nine		
right		
six		
time		
write		

G **Which word? Listen and circle.**

1	What	time / day	is it?
2	When is the	first / last	lesson?
3	Which	day / month	is it?
4	What's the	date / day	today?
5	I have three lessons this		evening. / morning.
6	This is my first		week. / year.

Lesson 4: Speaking

A **Look. Name the things.**

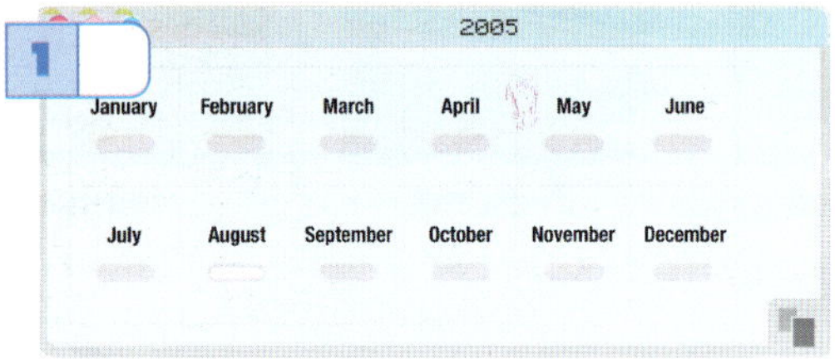

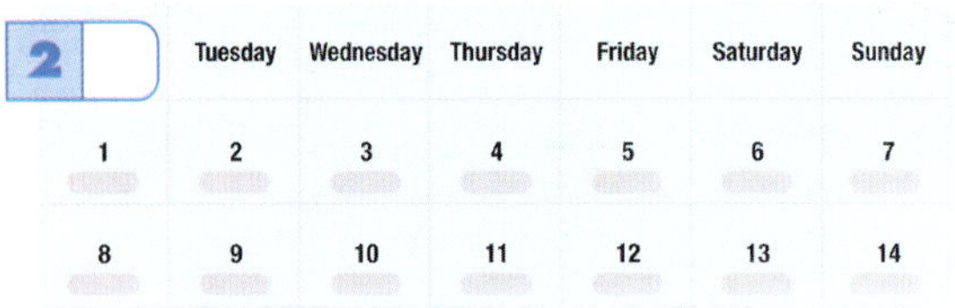

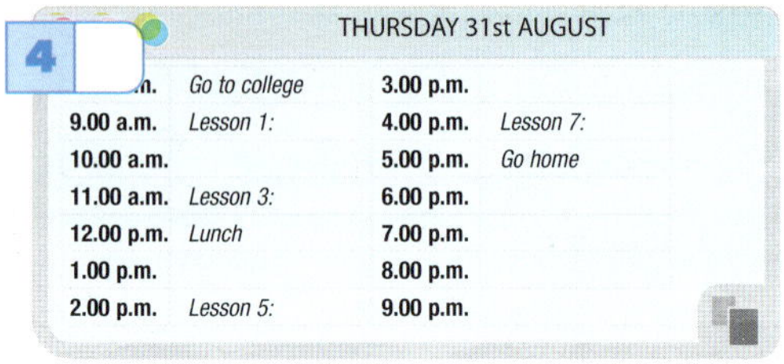

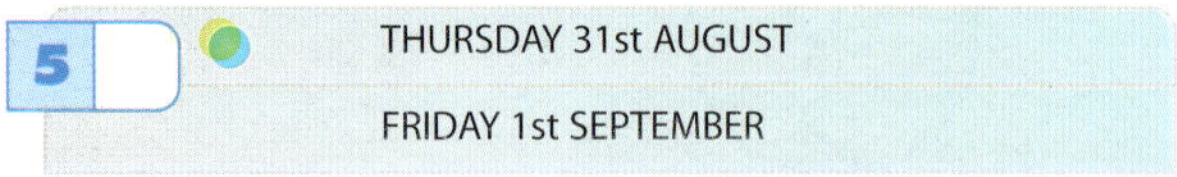

B **Listen and speak. Singular or plural?**

1 year

2 weeks

C **Look at the times.** ⇨

1 Greet your teacher.

2 Listen and answer.

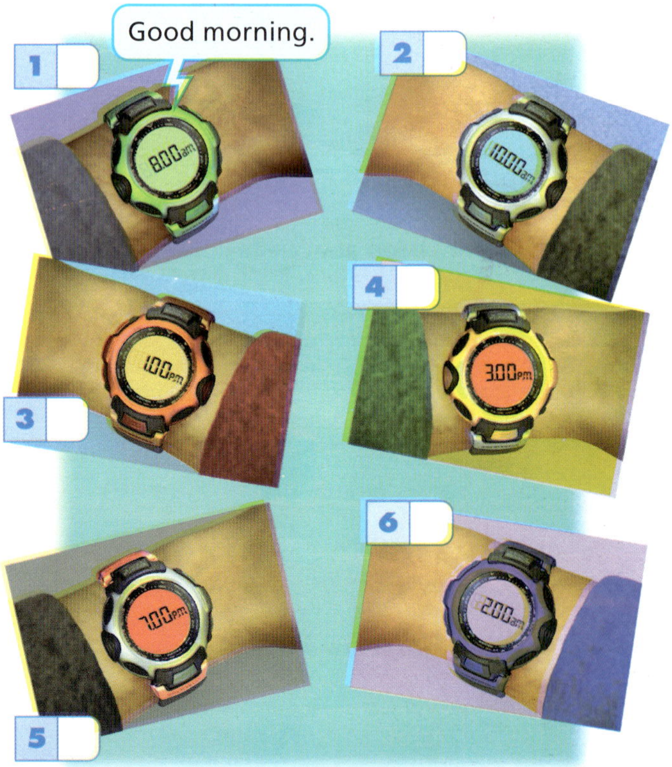

D **Read and ask.**

1 What's the …?

2 What's the … today?

3 When is the …?

4 Which … is it?

5 Where are you …?

E **Right or wrong? Listen and check.**

Lesson 4: Speaking

F Look at the pictures. ⇨

1 Listen.

2 Listen and answer.

3 Listen and ask.

G Work in pairs.

1 Ask and answer.
Student 1: You are the student.
Student 2: You are the teacher.

2 Swap roles.

Conversation 1

H Look at conversation 3. Work in pairs.

Ask and answer. Give true information.

Conversation 2

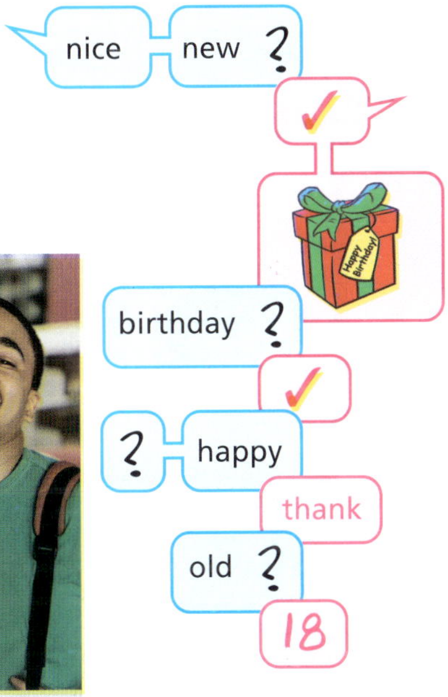

Conversation 3

I Listen. Complete the *Student* column of the table. Tick (✓) or cross (✗).

	Student	Me
	✓	

J Look at the table.

1 Complete the *Me* column. Tick (✓) or cross (✗).

2 Speak to the class.

Skills Check

Saying /ɪ/ and /aɪ/

Say each group of words.

/ɪ/	/aɪ/
it	I
in	fine
is	find
six	right
tick	write
fifteen	five
listen	night
begin	time

Guess the pronunciation of these words:
fin, shine, pile, bit, sight, lit, fight, dim.

THEME 1 Work and Business

Lesson 1: Listening

A Listen and point.

B Listen and do.

C Listen and answer.

D Right or wrong? Listen and check.

Lesson 2: Listening

A **Look at the five words.**

1 Listen and number.
2 Listen and write letters (A–E).
3 Listen and do.

court		
hospital		
office		
school		
bank		

B **Read.**

1 Listen and match.
2 Ask and answer.

Number 1: What does she do?
She's a doctor.

Number 2: What does he do?
He's a teacher.

Number 3: What do they do?
They're lawyers.

1 

4 

5 

2 

6 

3 

7 

- accountant
- doctor
- engineers
- lawyers
- programmers
- secretary
- teacher

C **Listen and tick (✓) the next word.**

1 26 ☐ doctor ☐ English ☑ Hospital ☐ Moscow ☐ Russian ☐
2 33 ☐ engineer ☐ factory ☐ French ☐ Japanese ☐ Paris ☐
3 Istanbul ☐ 45 ☐ Turkish ☐ bank ☐ accountant ☐
4 10.00 a.m. ☐ 29 ☐ court ☐ Italian ☐ lawyer ☐ Swiss ☐

D **Listen and complete the ID card.**

First name:	Jill
Family name:	
Nationality:	
Hometown:	
Job:	
Date of birth:	03/01/

Identity Card **Greenhill** College

E **Listen and answer.**

Skills Check

Hearing /ɑː/ and /eɪ/

Listen. Tick (✓) the correct column.

	/ɑː/ (*ask*)	/eɪ/ (*day*)
are		
class		
date		

What about *lawyer, have, what, factory, hospital, want, a?*

Lesson 3: Speaking

A **Look. Name the jobs and places.**

1

2

3

4

5

6

7

8

9

B **Listen to some sound effects.**

1 Listen. Identify the sounds.

2 Listen again. Who works here?

C **Choose an occupation.**

Ask and answer.

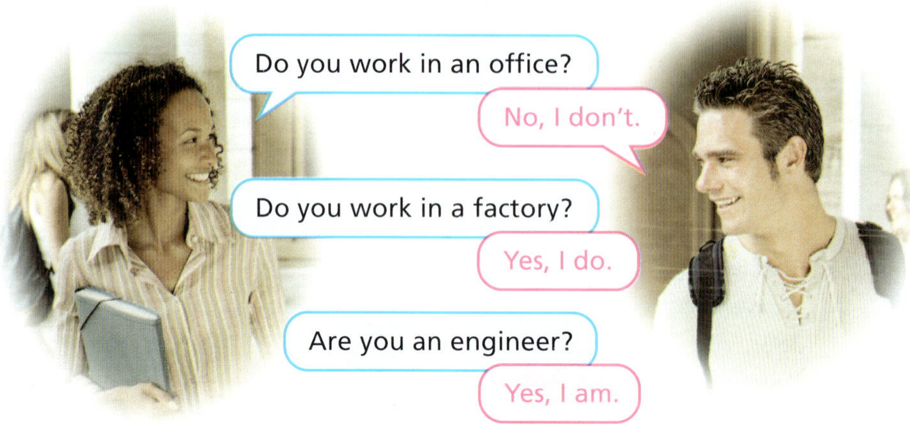

D **Ask and answer.**

What's your name?

1 what / name?

2 where / from?

3 how / old?

4 where / live?

5 what / do?

Lesson 4: Speaking

Conversation 1

Receptionist: Can I help you?
Carl Clark: I have a meeting with Mrs Dart.
Receptionist: What's your name, please?
Carl Clark: Carl Clark.
Receptionist: How do you spell that?
Carl Clark: C-A-R-L C-L-A-R-K.
Receptionist: Thank you, Mr Clark.

Receptionist: Mrs Dart? Mr Clark is here.
Mrs Dart: Thank you. Send him in.

A **Read and listen to conversation 1.**

1 Listen.

2 Listen and ask.

B **Work in pairs.**

Ask and answer. Give true information.

C **Look at conversations 2 a, b and c.**

1 Listen.

2 Listen and answer.

3 Listen and ask.

D **Work in pairs.**

1 Ask and answer.
Student 1: You are Carl.
Student 2: You are Mrs Dart.

2 Swap roles.

E **Look at the picture.**

1 Make sentences.

2 Listen and check.

F **Speak to the class.**

Conversation 2A

Conversation 2B

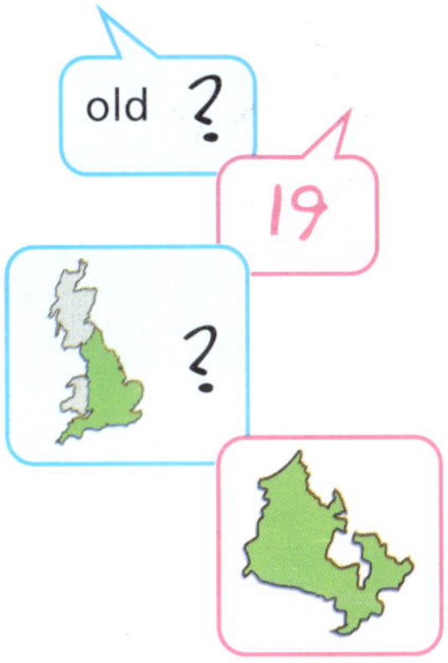

Conversation 2C

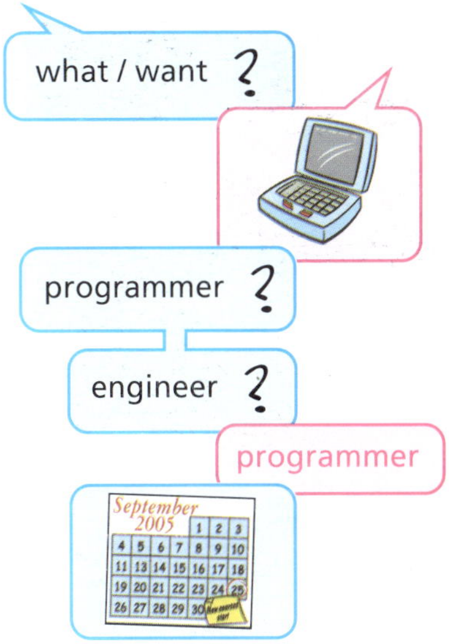

Skills Check

Saying /ɑː/ and /eɪ/

Say each group of words.

/ɑː/	/eɪ/
R	A
are	day
class	date
answer	name
ask	say
start	make
party	way
afternoon	play

THEME 2 Science and Nature

Lesson 1: Listening

A Listen and point.

B Listen and find.

C Listen and answer.

D Right or wrong? Listen and check.

Lesson 2: Listening

A Look. ⇨

1 Find two groups. Find the numbers of each group.

2 Listen and point.

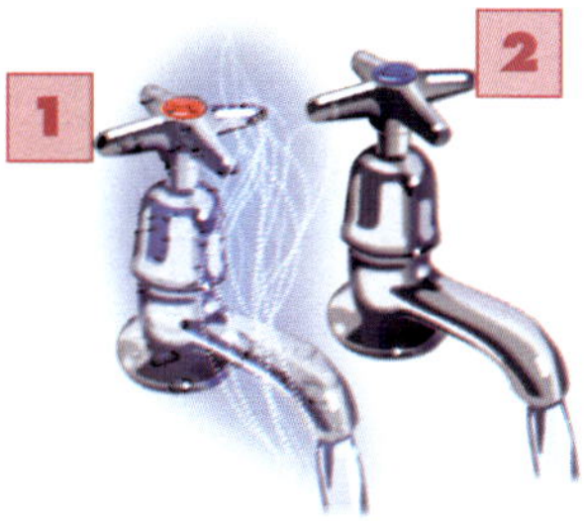

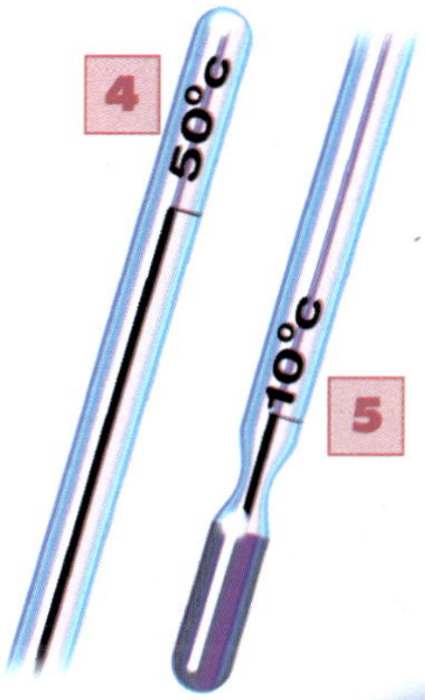

B Look and read. ⇨

1 Match.

2 Listen and check.

3 Ask and answer.

What is it?
It is snow.

What are they?
They are clouds.

What colour are they?
They are black.

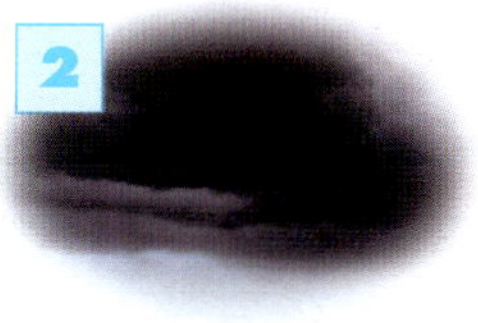

the sun
sand
snow
trees
clouds
grass

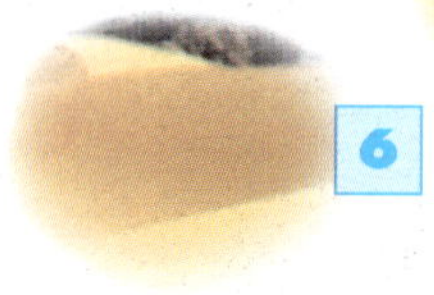

C Listen and draw.

D Listen. Find and number six items in the picture in Lesson 1.

E Listen. What is it?

Skills Check 1

Revision

~~grass~~ grey red white sky yellow

Say these words from this theme.

Write each word under the correct vowel sound.

/e/	/aɪ/	/ɑː/	/eɪ/
(pen)	(five)	(ask)	(date)
		grass	

Listen and check.

Skills Check 2

Hearing /iː/

Listen. Tick (✓) the words with /iː/.

tree		he		she	
blue		grey		we	
green		see		the	

Lesson 3: Speaking

A **Look at the drawings. How many …**

1 red squares?

2 grey squares?

3 black squares?

4 green circles?

B **Listen. Which drawing is it?**

C **Work in pairs.**

1 Talk about each drawing. What can you see?

2 Choose a drawing. Describe it. Can your partner identify the drawing?

1

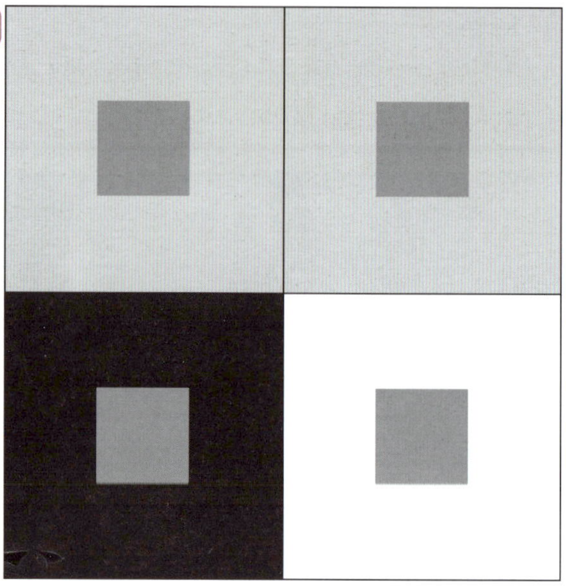

2

3

4

5

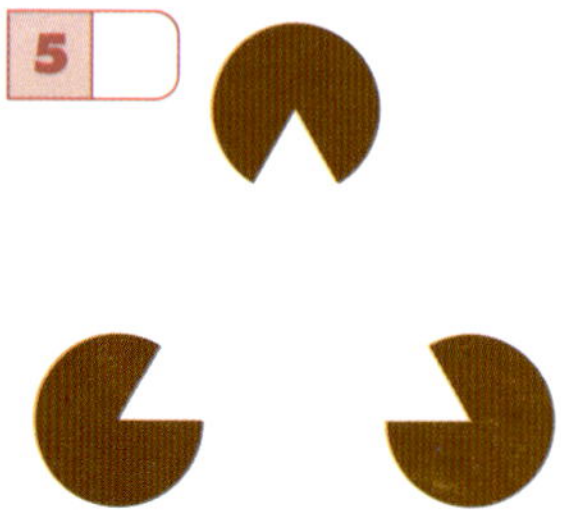

6

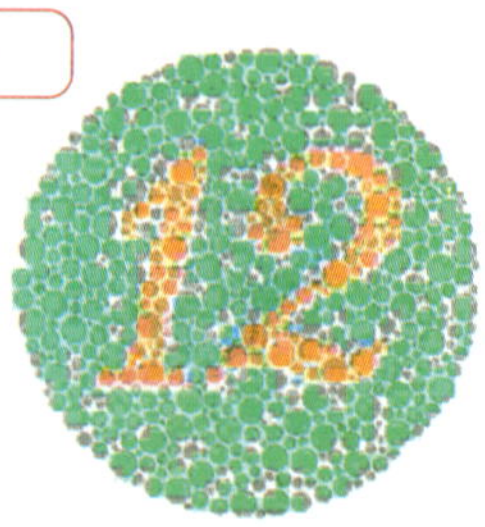

7

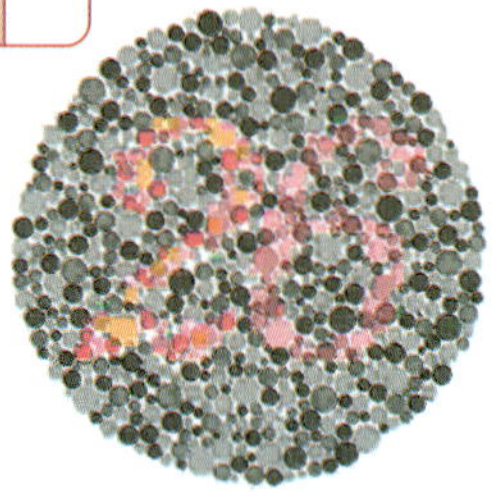

8

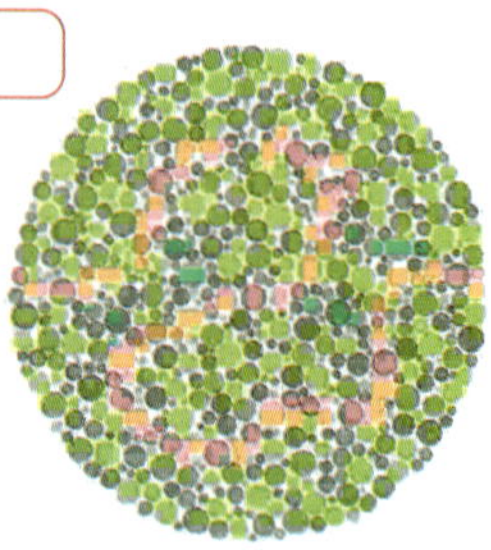

Lesson 4: Speaking

Conversation 1

Lee: Look at this drawing.
Kim: Which drawing?
Lee: This one. Number 2. What can you see?
Kim: I can see black squares.
Lee: What else can you see?
Kim: There are lines. What is this colour?
Lee: It's grey.
Kim: How do you say the word?
Lee: Grey.
Kim: Grey. OK. There are grey lines.
Lee: Anything else?
Kim: Oh, yes. I can see white circles.
Lee: How many circles are there?
Kim: There are … I can't count them! They change from white to black! I don't understand. Why do they do that?

Conversation 2

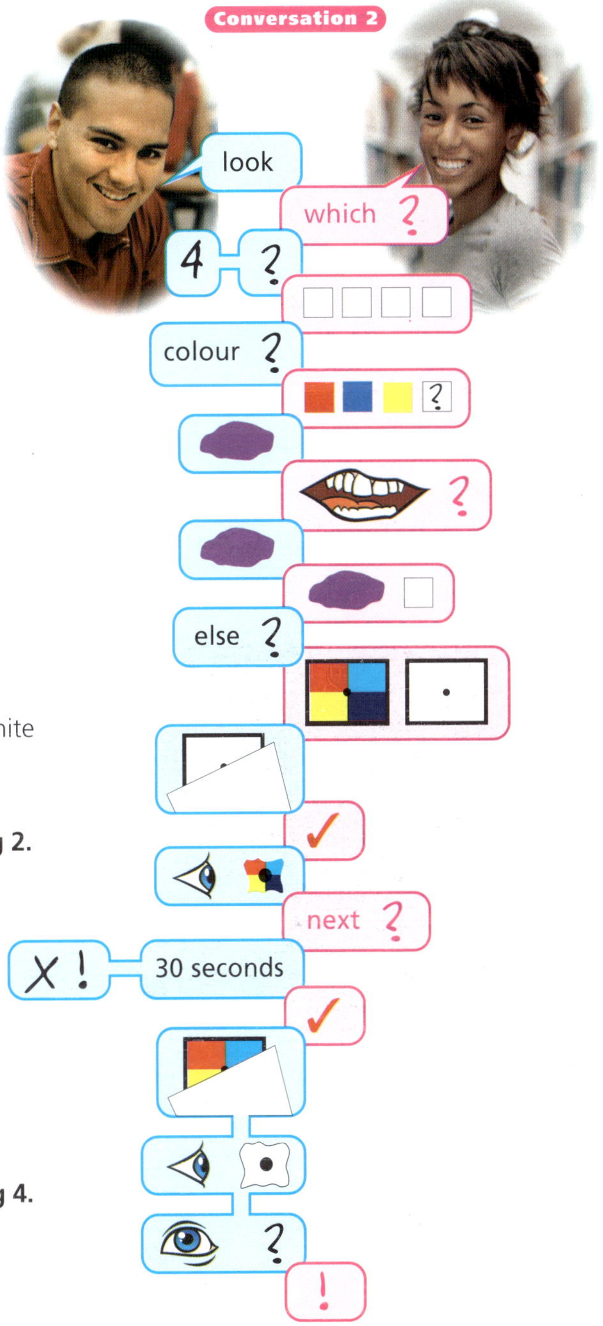

A **You are going to hear a conversation about drawing 2.**

1 Look at the drawing. What can you see?
2 Listen.
3 Listen and read.
4 Listen and answer.

B **Read conversation 1 in pairs.**

C **You are going to hear a conversation about drawing 4.**

1 Look at the drawing. What can you see?
2 Listen.

D **Role-play conversation 2 in pairs.**

E **Choose another drawing.**

1 What can you see?
2 Explain it to your partner.

F **Why does it happen? Explain the strange thing about your drawing.**

Skills Check

Saying *can* and *can't*

- The vowel in *can* is short.
- The vowel in *can't* is long.
  Use a long vowel with the negative.

Find sentences with *can* and *can't*.
Practise saying the sentences.

Lesson 1: Listening

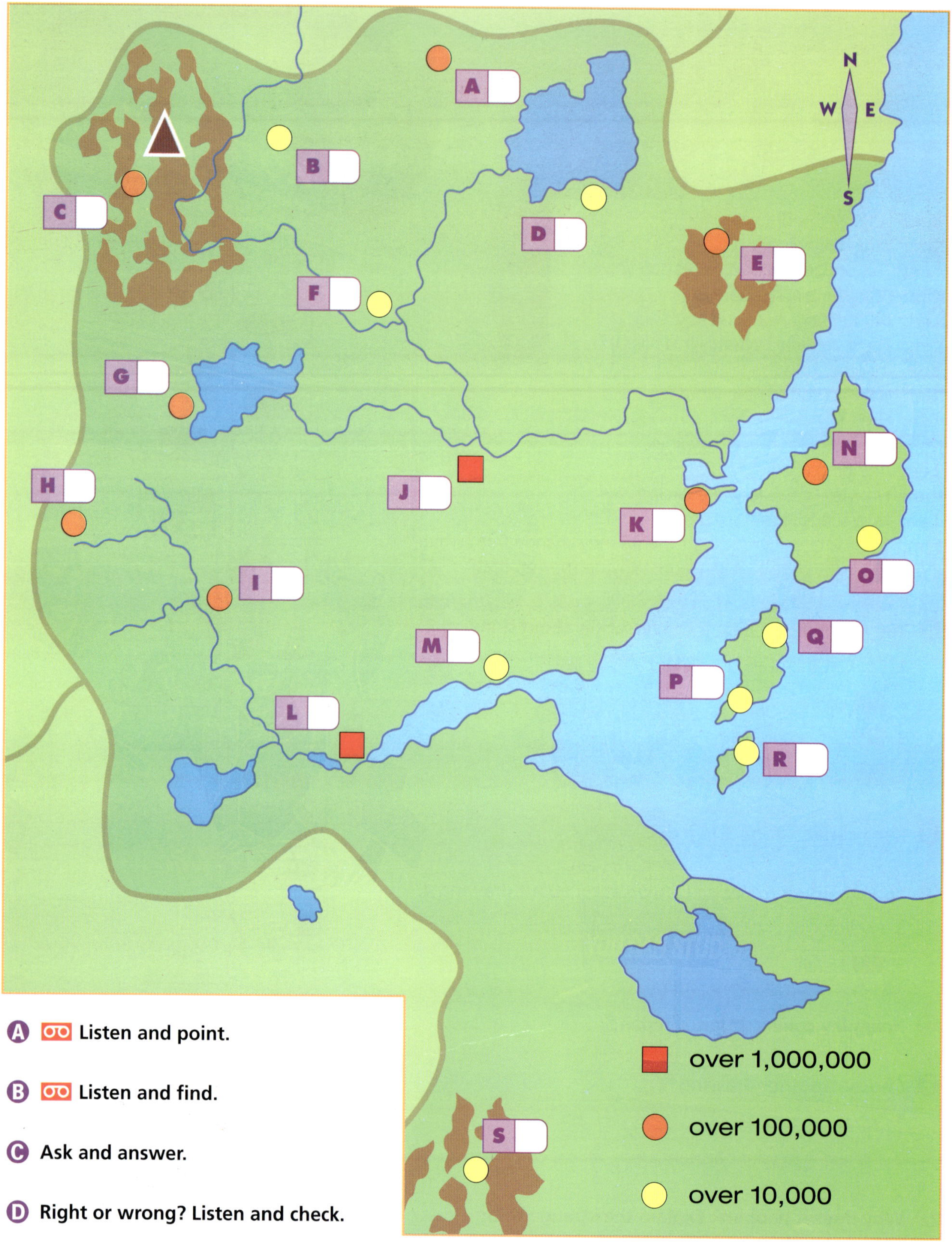

A Listen and point.

B Listen and find.

C Ask and answer.

D Right or wrong? Listen and check.

Lesson 2: Listening

Lake

City

Mountains

River

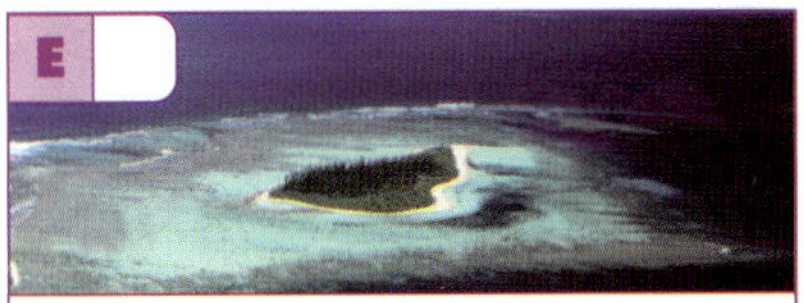

Island

Ⓐ Look. ⇧

1 Listen and number.

2 Listen and answer.

Ⓑ Read.

1 Listen and number.

2 Remember the words.

coast	
cold	
country	1
east	
hot	
north	
south	
town	
village	
west	

Ⓒ Listen and draw.

Skills Check 1

Revision

~~west~~ river east island lake
left city right centre village

Say these words from this theme.

Write each word under the correct vowel sound.

Listen and check.

/e/ (pen)	/ɪ/ (six)	/iː/ (tree)	/aɪ/ (five)	/eɪ/ (date)
west				

Skills Check 2

Hearing /aʊ/

Listen. Tick (✓) the words with /aʊ/.

south		brown	
town		around	
country		snow	
mountain		yellow	
coast		accountant	
hour		cloud	
now		cold	

Lesson 3: Speaking

A Look.

1 Name the places.

2 Where is each picture?

3 Close your book. Can you remember the eight pictures?

B Listen and repeat.

C Choose a place.

Ask and answer.

D Ask and answer.

1 come from?

2 city?

3 where?

4 coast?

5 islands?

6 rivers?

7 mountains / your country?

8 lakes?

Lesson 4: Speaking

A Role-play.

Ask and answer about your partner's country.

Student 1: You come from Athens in Greece.

Student 2: You come from Caracas in Venezuela.

B Read and do.

1 Draw an outline map of your country or your area in the left box at the bottom of the page.

2 Add the main cities and towns.

3 Add the mountains, the rivers, the lakes and the islands.

4 Label the items.

C Work in pairs.

Do not show your map to your partner!

1 Draw an outline map of your country or area in your partner's book. Use the box on the right.

2 Describe your map.

3 Complete the map of your partner's country or area.

Skills Check

Saying /aʊ/

Say these words.

town	brown
cloud	around
hour	mountain
now	accountant

What about snow, yellow, country, know?

Lesson 1: Listening

1

2

3

4

A Listen and point.

B Listen and find.

C Listen and answer.

D Listen. True or false?

E Right or wrong?
Listen and check.

Lesson 2: Listening

A

Baby

B
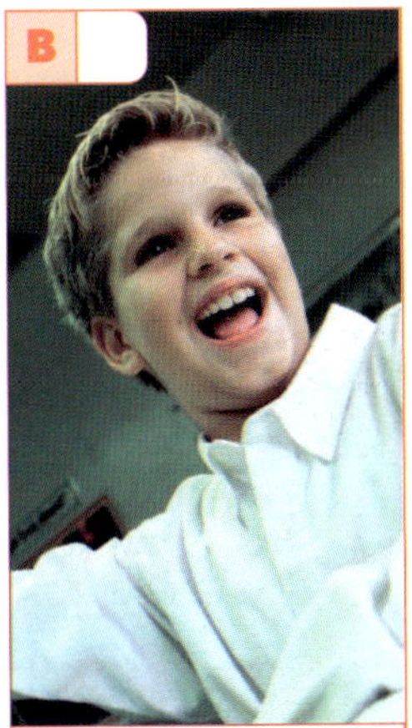
Child

C

Teenager

D

Adult

E

Old person

A Look. ⇧

1 Listen and number.
2 Listen and answer.
3 Cover and remember.

B Look and read.

1 Match. ⇩
2 Listen and check.
3 Ask and answer.

What do you have for *baby*?

0 to 2.

I do, too.

Age	
100	adult
90	
80	
70	old person
60	
50	
40	baby
30	
20	
15	child
10	
5	
0	teenager

Skills Check 1

Revision

men female women child teenager male people children friend baby

Write each word under the correct vowel sound.

/e/	/ɪ/	/iː/	/aɪ/	/eɪ/
(ten)	(six)	(three)	(five)	(eight)

Listen and check.

Skills Check 2

Hearing /æ/

Listen. Tick (✓) the words with /æ/.

adult		male	
ask		lake	
last		woman	
can		man	
can't		map	
Saturday		village	

Lesson 3: Speaking

A **Look at the photographs. How many …**

1 women? 4 boys? 7 babies?
2 men? 5 adults? 8 males?
3 girls? 6 children? 9 females?

B **Listen. Which photograph is it?**

That's number 3.

Yes, I agree.

I think it's number 1.

Do you? I don't. I think it's number 6.

C **Work in pairs.**

1 Talk about each photograph. What can you see?
2 Choose a photograph. Describe it. Can your partner identify the photograph?

Lesson 4: Speaking

A You will hear a conversation about words.

1 Look at the conversation and listen.

2 Ask the questions.

B Work in pairs. Ask and answer.

C Read Skills Check 1. How do you ask about …

1 spelling?

2 pronunciation?

3 stress?

4 meaning?

D Where is the stress in these words? ⇩

1 Say the words in your head.

2 Mark the stress.

3 Listen and check your answers.

4 Look the words up in a dictionary and check.

Syllables	
1st	2nd
ˈa	dult
peo	ple
wo	man
wo	men

Syllables	
1st	2nd
chil	dren
ba	bies
per	son
cul	ture

E Look back through this book. Ask and answer about words.

Skills Check 1

Asking about new words

• spelling	How do you **spell** …?
• pronunciation	How do you **say** this word?
• stress	Where is the **stress** in this word?
• meaning	What does … **mean**?

Skills Check 2

The letter *a*

• This letter makes many vowel sounds.

Examples:

man map has have adult

last ask answer start

say day way date name

Learn the sound of *a* in a new word.

Lesson 1: Listening

A Listen and point.

B Listen and complete the table.

C Listen and answer.

D Listen. True or false?

E Listen and check.

Table 1: *How do people get to work in New Zealand?*

Method	Number	%

others		
Total	1,231,000	

Lesson 2: Listening

Fly

Drive

Ride

Sail

Walk

A Look.

1. Listen and number.
2. Listen and answer.
3. Cover and remember.

B Look at Table 2.

1. Think and predict.
2. Listen and check.
3. Ask and answer.

What speed do you have for *plane*?

7,692.66.

I do, too. What date do you have?

The twenty-eighth of February, 2004.

Really? I have the twenty-eighth of March.

Table 2: *Record speeds*

	Speed (in kph)	Date
plane		
car		
motorbike		
train		
bicycle		

Source: Guinness World Records 2005

268.83	18/05/90
1,227.98	15/10/97
43.67	3/10/95
674.28	24/09/67
515.30	14/07/90
7,692.66	28/03/04
518.45	10/06/84

Skills Check 1

Predicting information

- Before you listen to a lecture, think: *What is the lecturer going to say?*

Skills Check 2

Revision

bicycle drive fly plane sail ship street train track motorbike

Write each word under the correct vowel sound.

/ɪ/ (six)	/iː/ (tree)	/aɪ/ (five)	/æ/ (map)	/eɪ/ (date)

Listen and check.

Skills Check 3

Hearing /əʊ/

Listen. Tick (✓) the words with /əʊ/.

boat	✓	goes		no	
do		motor		now	
does		home		road	
don't		how		phone	
go		know		long	

Lesson 3: Speaking

A Look. ⇧

1 Name the things.

2 Where is each thing?

B Listen. What is it?

C Read and listen to the conversation.

1 Listen.

2 Listen and answer.

D Work in pairs.

1 Ask and answer. Give true information.

2 Talk about your partner.

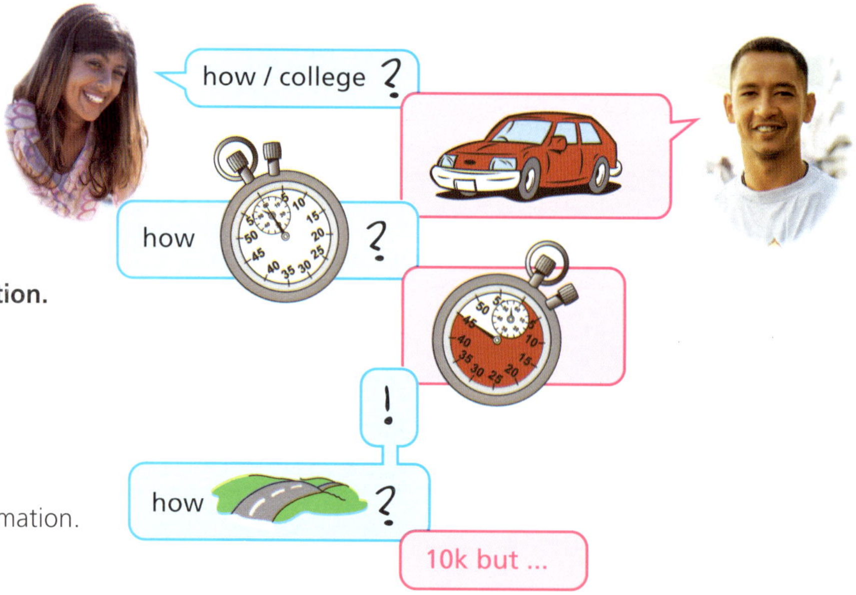

Lesson 4: Speaking

Figure 1: ***How do people get to work in Melbourne, Australia?***

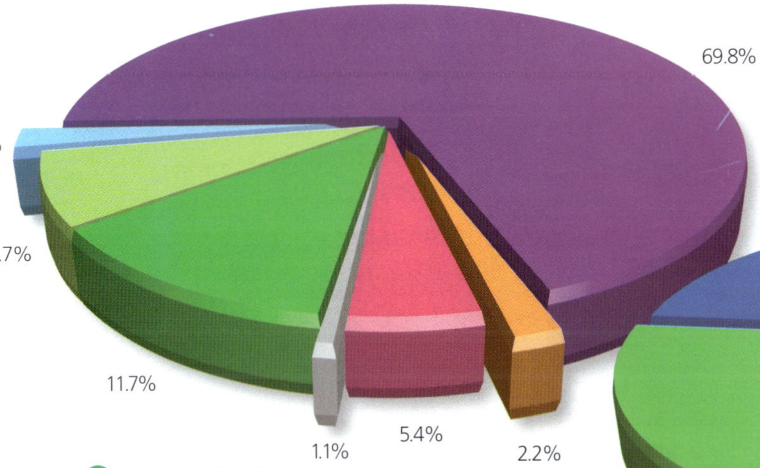

Figure 2: ***How do people get to work in London, UK?***

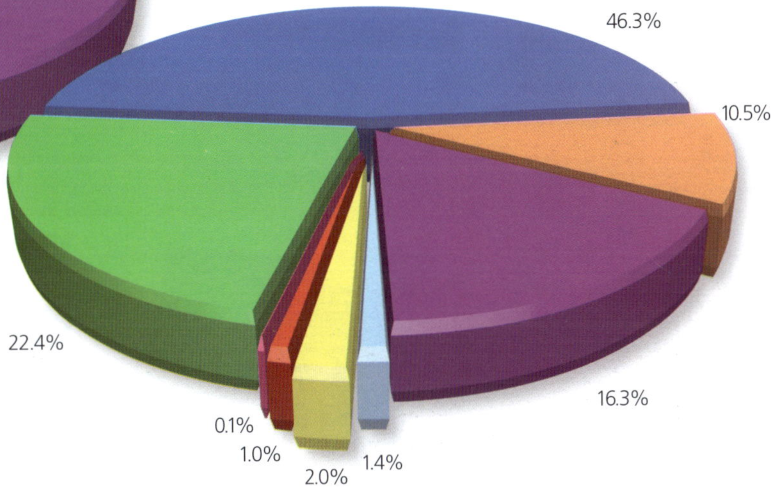

Key

Underground	train	walk	
motorbike	bicycle	taxi	other
bus	tram	car	

A Study the figures.

1 Answer the questions.

2 Ask and answer in pairs.

B Marc and Simone are talking about the figures. Listen.

1 What is a tram?

2 What is the Underground?

3 How do you say each word?

C Work in pairs.

1 Choose one of the figures each. Cover the other figure.

2 Dictate the information from your figure to your partner.

3 Write the information you hear in Table 1 or Table 2 below.

Table 1: ***How do people get to work in Melbourne, Australia?***

Method	%
car	
train	
tram	
walk	
bus	
bicycle	
other	

Table 2: ***How do people get to work in London, UK?***

Method	%
underground	
train	
car	
bus	
motorbike	
bicycle	
taxi	
walk	

Skills Check 1

Defining things

- We often define things with a general word then a fact.

Example:

A tram is a kind of **bus**.

It goes on tracks on the road.

Skills Check 2

Saying /əʊ/ and /aʊ/

Say each group of words.

/əʊ/	boat motor road go
/aʊ/	how now ground cloud

How do you say:

snow, know, don't, brown, yellow?

Lesson 1: Listening

A

B

C

D

I remember, I remember,
The house where I was born,
The little window where the sun
Came peeping in at morn;
He never came a wink too soon,
Nor brought too long a day,
But now, I often wish the night
Had borne my breath away!

THOMAS HOOD (1799–1845)

E

F

G

H

I

J

Thomas Hood was born in London in 1799. He was the son of a bookseller. His father died in 1811. He had to leave school and get a job. He started writing at the age of 22

K

A Listen and circle or box.

B Listen and point.

C Listen to the lecture. Number the paintings.

D Listen and answer.

Skills Check

Preparing to listen

- Lecturers usually begin with an introduction. The introduction gives you a general idea of the content. Listen carefully to it. Think: *What words am I going to hear in this lecture?*

Lesson 2: Listening

A Look. ⇧

1 Find two groups.

2 Listen and check.

3 Name the two groups.

B What are the job names?

1 Discuss in pairs.

2 Listen and check.

What did she call this kind of artist?

I think she said painter.

How do you spell that?

I don't know. Maybe it's P-A-I-N-T-E-R or P-A-I-N-T-O-R.

C What is the connection between all the words in the box? (Clue: Think about sounds.)

writer	painter	sculptor	literature
biographer	sculpture	architecture	

1 Work in pairs. Find a connection.

2 Listen and check.

3 Read Skills Check 2 and check.

4 Can you see any patterns?

Skills Check 1

Guessing information

- You often hear new words in a lecture. Write something down, then check with your friends.

Skills Check 2

Hearing /ə/ at the end of words

- Many words in English end in the /ə/ sound.

Examples:

writ**er** paint**er** biograph**er**
sculpt**or** doct**or** profess**or**
litera**ture** sculp**ture** architec**ture**

Skills Check 3

Revision

literature seascape writer poet still
life kind painter art landscape
play architect portrait

Write each word under the correct vowel sound.

/ɪ/ (six)	/iː/ (three)	/aɪ/ (five)	/əʊ/ (boat)

/eɪ/ (eight)	/ɑː/ (car)	/æ/ (map)

Listen and check.

1

2

3

4

5

Shall I compare thee to a summer's day?
Thou art more lovely and more temperate.
Rough winds do shake the darling buds of May,
And summer's lease hath all too short a date.

6

Charles Dickens was born on February 7th, 1812, in Portsmouth in the south of England.

7

8

9

10

A Look. ⇧

1 How many pieces of literature are there?

2 How many pieces of art are there?

3 Name the items.

B Ask and answer about the items. ⇨

What's this?

It's a piece of architecture.

Do you like it?

Yes, I do.

What do you call this kind of painting?

It's a landscape.

What do you think of it?

I don't like it.

C Who wrote, painted or made each piece of art or literature?

Example: *Number 1 a painter*

D Work in pairs.

Student 1: Close your book. Answer questions about the art and literature on this page.

Student 2: Test Student 1 on the art and literature on this page.

Skills Check

Saying /ə/ at the end of words

- Many words in English end in the /ə/ sound.

Examples:

writ**er** paint**er** biograph**er**

sculpt**or** doct**or**

pict**ure** sculpt**ure** literat**ure**

Say each word. Make the /ə/ sound at the end.

Lesson 4: Speaking

Conversation 1

Andy: Who is the most famous writer in your culture?
Hosni: I think it's Naguib Mahfouz.
Andy: Is that a man or a woman?
Hosni: It's a man.
Andy: How do you spell his name?
Hosni: N-A-G-U-I-B M-A-H-F-O-U-Z.
Andy: Is he alive or dead?
Hosni: He's still alive, but he's very old.
Andy: When was he born?
Hosni: I think it was about 1911.
Andy: Did he work as a writer?
Hosni: No. He worked for the Egyptian government.
Andy: What kind of literature does he write?
Hosni: Novels and short stories. He wrote three books called *The Cairo Trilogy*.
Andy: Where does he live?
Hosni: In Cairo.

Conversation 2

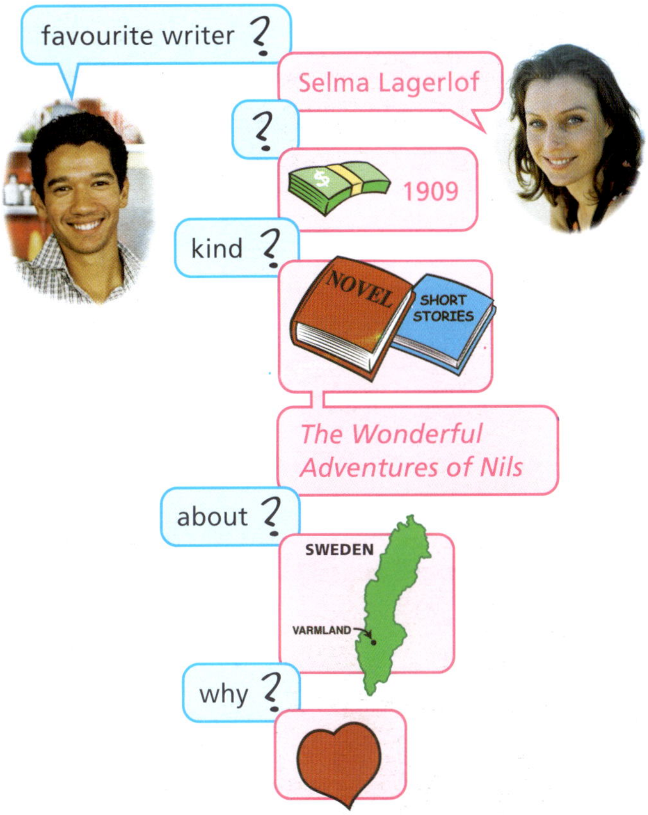

A **Read and listen to conversation 1.**

1. Listen.
2. Listen and ask.
3. Listen and answer.

B **Look at conversation 2.**

1. Try to work it out from the words and pictures.
2. Listen and check.
3. Listen and answer.
4. Listen and ask.

C **What is the past tense form of these verbs?**

answer ask be end listen live look
play talk test win work write

1. Say the words.
2. Read the Skills Check and check.

D **Work in pairs. Have a conversation about your favourite writer.**

E **Write a short talk about the most famous writer in your culture. Give your talk in small groups.**

Skills Check

Talking about the past

- The past form of most verbs is (e)*d*.
  Examples:
  She liv**ed** in Varmland.
  He work**ed** for the government.
- The final sound is usually /t/ or /d/, but if the verbs end in *t* or *d*, we make the past form with /ɪd/.
  Examples:
  end**ed** test**ed**
- Many verbs have a special past form for the past tense.
  Examples:

be	He **was** born in 1911.
write	She **wrote** novels.
win	She **won** the Nobel Prize in 1909.

Lesson 1: Listening

A Listen and circle or box.

B Listen and point.

C Listen. *What am I doing?*

D Listen and complete the table.

E Listen. True or false?

F Work in pairs. The table shows the most popular activities for adults in the UK. Are the figures correct for you?

Table 1: *Most popular leisure activities for adults in the UK*

Activity	Minutes per day
TV/films	
meeting friends	
playing sports	
playing games	
listening to the radio/music	
Total	**306**

Lesson 2: Listening

A

Cinema

B

Stadium

C

Theatre

D

Mall

E

Sports centre

A Look. ⇧

1. Listen and number.
2. Listen and answer.
3. Cover and remember.

B Ask and answer.

Student 1: Choose a picture from Lesson 1 or Lesson 2. Answer Student 2's questions.

Student 2: Ask *Yes/No* questions. Find the correct picture.

Are there a lot of people in the picture?

Yes, there are.

Are they sitting?

Yes, they are.

Are they watching football?

No, they aren't.

Are they at a cinema?

Yes, they are.

Is it the picture top left?

Yes, it is.

C Listen to the first part of a lecture.

1. What is the lecturer going to talk about?
2. When the lecturer stops, say the next word.

Skills Check 1

Predicting the next word or phrase

- When we listen, we can often predict the next word or phrase. This helps with active listening. Think: *What is the lecturer going to say next?*

Skills Check 2

Hearing /ɒ/ and /ɔː/

Listen. Tick ( ) the correct column.

	/ɒ/ (hot)	/ɔː/ (call)
ball		
job		
watch		
what		
mall		
orange		
sport		
walk		
want		

What about *work, world, word*

Lesson 3: Speaking

1

2

3

4

5

6
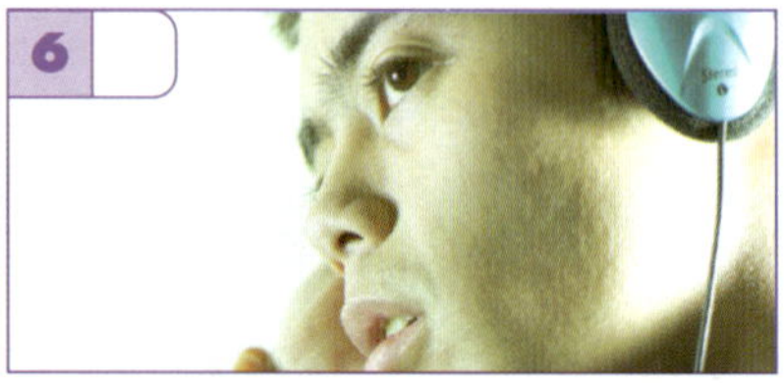
7

8

9

10

11

12

13

A Look. ⇧

1 Name the sports.

2 Name the other leisure activities.

3 Name the places.

B Work in pairs.

Student 1: Cover the pictures. How many can you describe to your partner?

Student 2: Check your partner's descriptions.

C Look at the conversation. ⇨

1 Listen.

2 Listen and answer.

D Work in pairs.

1 Ask and answer. Give true information.

2 Talk about your partner.

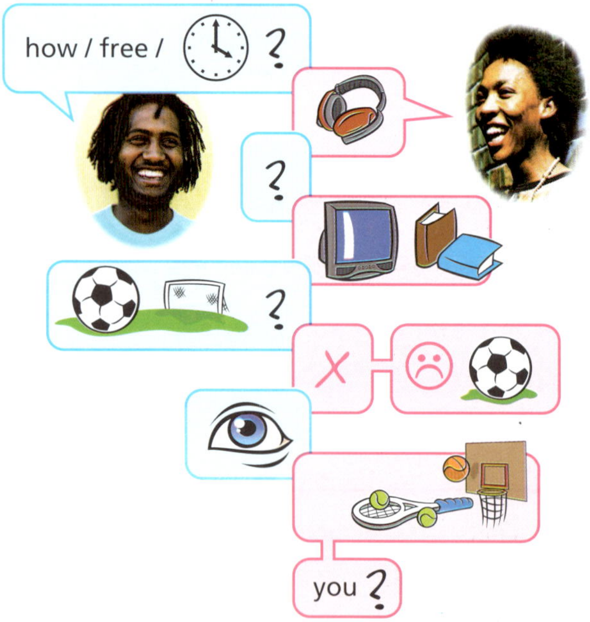

Lesson 4: Speaking

Figure 1: *Favourite leisure activities for children (11–15) in Ontario, Canada*

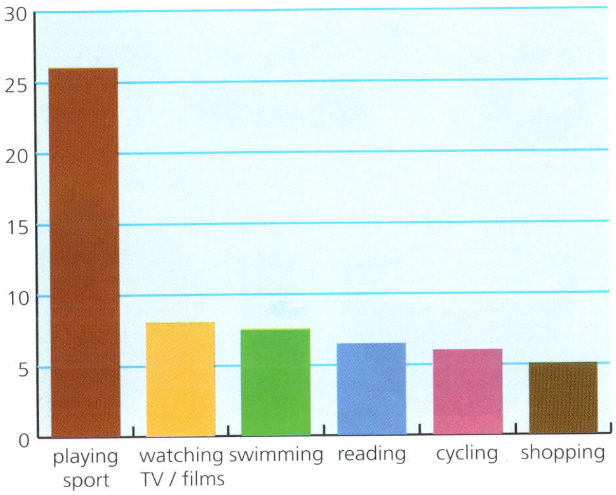

Figure 2: *Favourite leisure activities for teenagers (16–20) in Ontario, Canada*

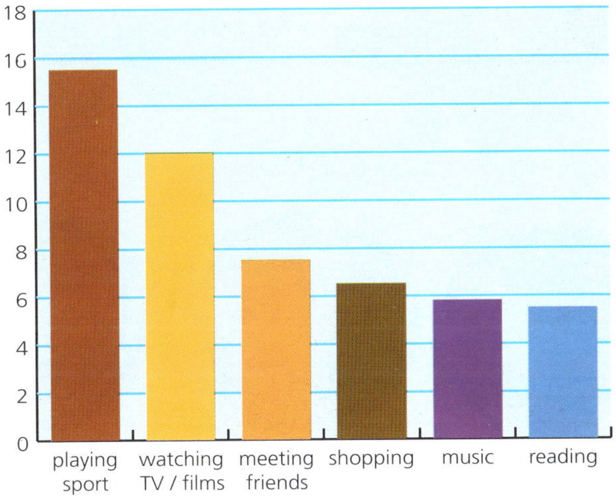

A Study the figures.

1 Answer the questions.

2 Ask and answer in pairs.

B Françoise and Pierre are talking about Figure 2. Listen and write each percentage in the correct place.

C Work in pairs.

1 Choose one of the figures each. Cover the other figure.

2 Dictate the information from your figure to your partner.

3 Write the information you hear in Table 1 or Table 2 below.

Skills Check 1

Talking about figures

- Figures show us a picture of information. They often do not give the exact number.

  Examples:

  Just under eight percent of 16- to 20-year-olds chose meeting friends.

  Just over six percent said shopping.

Skills Check 2

Saying /ɒ/ and /ɔː/

Say each group of words.

/ɒ/	not what watch was shopping
/ɔː/	sport call fourth saw

Table 1: *Most popular leisure activities for teenagers (16–20) in Ontario, Canada*

Method	%
meeting friends	
music	
playing sport	
reading	
shopping	
watching TV/films	

Table 2: *Most popular leisure activities for children (11–15) in Ontario, Canada*

Method	%
cycling	
playing sport	
reading	
shopping	
swimming	
watching TV/films	

Lesson 1: Listening

A

B

C

D

E

F

G

H

I

J

K

L

M

N

O

P

Q
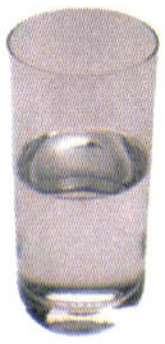

A Listen and circle or box.

B Listen and point.

C Listen and answer.

D Listen and complete the table.

E Ask and answer about items in the table.

Table 1: *Energy value of certain food and drinks*

Food/Drink	Calories	Quantity
	270	one, with skin
	210	one portion
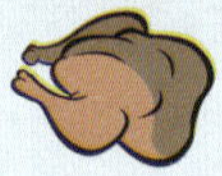		one piece
		one piece
		one cone
		one glass
	125	one piece
		one can
	90	one
		on one piece of bread
		one spoon

Lesson 2: Listening

A **Look.** ⇧

1. What is the group word for each kind of food?
2. Which kinds of food above give you energy?
3. What other kinds of food give you energy?
4. Listen and write.
5. Remember and number the kinds of food.

B **Listen and complete Table 1.**

Table 1: ***Average daily calorie consumption by food source***

	Calories
cereals	
sugar	232
potatoes	
vegetables	75
fruit	
milk	30
Total	

C **Listen and label Figure 1.**

Figure 1: ***Average daily calorie consumption by food source***

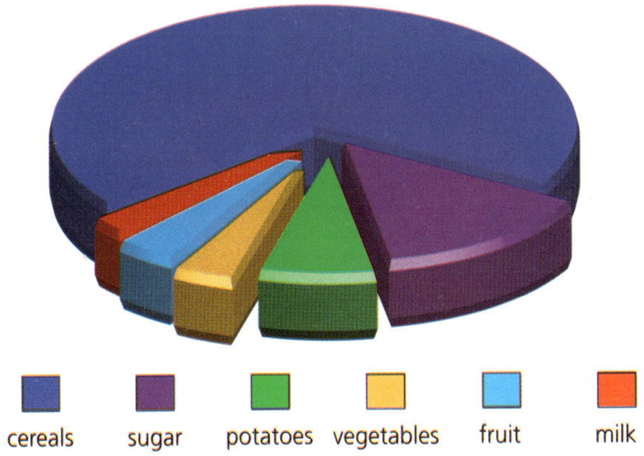

Skills Check 1

Listening for examples

- Lecturers often give examples of new words. If you do not understand a new word, listen for any examples. Perhaps they will help you to understand.

  Example:

  The biggest source of energy is **cereals**.
  Cereals are kinds of **food**, like **bread**, **pasta** and **rice**.

Skills Check 2

Hearing /uː/ and /ʊ/

Listen. Tick (✓) the correct column.

	/uː/ (food)	/ʊ/ (good)
fruit		
blue		
book		
cook		
could		
do		
juice		
look		
new		
sugar		
would		

What about these words *build, our, does, go*

Lesson 3: Speaking

Conversation 1

Conversation 2

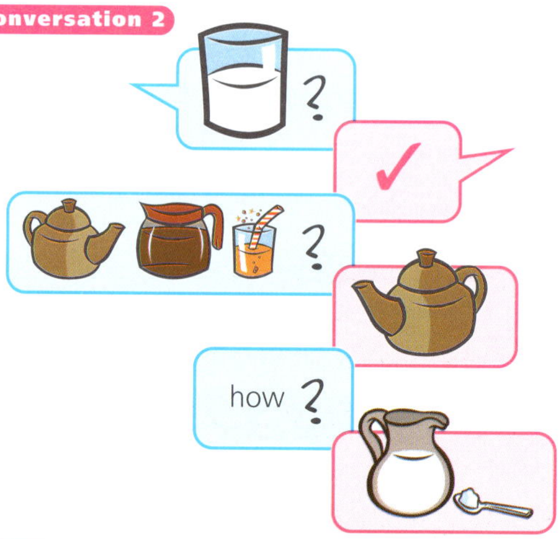

Conversation 3

A Look at the pictures for two minutes.

1 Cover the pictures.

2 Name the food items.

3 Name the drinks.

4 Are there any vegetables in the picture? What about fruit?

B Look at each conversation.

1 What are they saying?

2 Listen and check.

3 Listen and answer.

4 Ask and answer in pairs.

C Work in pairs.

Student 1: Offer your partner a drink. Choose some food.

Student 2: Choose a drink. Offer your partner some food.

Lesson 4: Speaking

Table 1: *Consumption of drinks, Canada, 1997*

Amount per person p.a.	
Drink	**Litres**
soft drinks	112.6
coffee	93.7
milk	
tea	
fruit juice	
bottled water	21.4
vegetable juice	
Total	**402.3**

Figure 1: *Consumption of drinks, Canada, 1997*

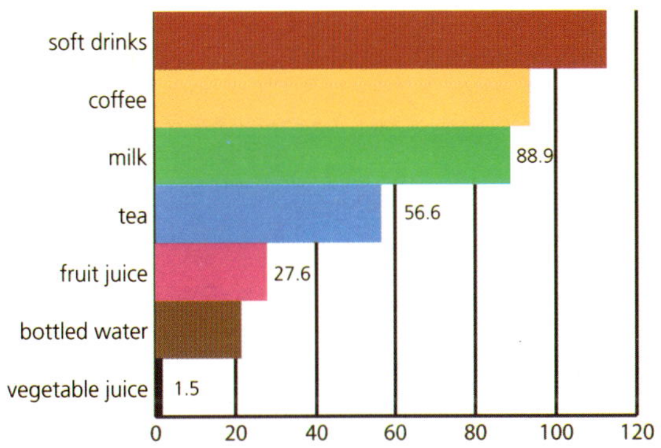

A Study Table 1 and Figure 1.

1 Answer the questions.

2 Ask and answer to complete. Work in pairs

Student 1: Cover Figure 1. Ask Student 2 for the missing information.

Student 2: Cover Table 1. Ask Student 1 for the missing information.

How much tea did Canadians drink in 1997?

Fifty-six point six litres. How many soft drinks did they have?

B Work in groups of four.

1 Ask each other questions to complete the chart below.

2 Make a bar chart from the answers.

Skills Check 1

Doing research

- Make a chart before you start asking research questions.

Example:

Drink	S1	S2	S3	S4	Total
soft drinks	4	3	0	5	12

Skills Check 2

Saying /uː/ and /ʊ/

Say each group of words.

/uː/	/ʊ/
fruit	good
juice	cook
to	look
food	would
do	could

Drink	S1	S2	S3	S4	Total
soft drinks					
coffee					
milk					
tea					
fruit juice					
bottled water					
vegetable juice					

Word Lists: Thematic

STARTER

afternoon *(n)*
answer *(n and v)*
ask *(v)*
begin *(v)*
day *(n)*
end *(v)*
evening *(n)*
first *(adj)*
hour *(n)*
last *(adj)*
listen *(v)*
month *(n)*
morning *(n)*
night *(n)*
now *(adv)*
question *(n)*
read *(v)*
right *(adj)*
student *(n)*
test *(n and v)*
time *(n)*
today *(n)*
week *(n)*
write *(v)*
wrong *(adj)*
year *(n)*

THEME 1
Work and Business

accountant *(n)*
bank *(n)*
computer *(n)*
court *(n)*
doctor *(n)*
engineer *(v)*
factory *(v)*
hospital *(n)*
hotel *(n)*
job *(n)*
lawyer *(n)*
office *(n)*
receptionist *(n)*
secretary *(n)*
shop *(n)*
start *(v)*
typist *(n)*
want *(v)*
work *(n and v)*

THEME 2
Science and Nature

black *(adj)*
blue *(adj)*
brown *(adj)*
cloud *(n)*
cold *(adj)*
colour *(n and v)*
grass *(n)*
green *(adj)*
grey *(adj)*
hot *(adj)*
orange *(adj)*
red *(adj)*
sky *(n)*
snow *(n)*
sun *(n)*
tree *(n)*
white *(adj)*
yellow *(adj)*

THEME 3
The Physical World

bottom *(n)*
centre *(n)*
coast *(n)*
country *(n)*
east *(n)*
island *(n)*
lake *(n)*
left *(adj)*
map *(n)*
mountain *(n)*
north *(n)*
river *(n)*
south *(n)*
top *(n)*
town *(n)*
village *(n)*
west *(n)*

THEME 4
Culture and Civilization

adult *(n)*

baby *(n)*

boy *(n)*

child *(n)*

female *(adj)*

friend *(n)*

girl *(n)*

male *(adj)*

man *(n)*

old *(adj)*

people *(n)*

person *(n)*

teenager *(n)*

woman *(n)*

young *(adj)*

THEME 5
They Made Our World

bicycle *(n)*

boat *(n)*

bus *(n)*

car *(n)*

come *(v)*

drive *(v)*

fly *(v)*

go *(v)*

motorbike *(n)*

plane *(n)*

road *(n)*

sail *(v)*

ship *(n)*

taxi *(n)*

train *(n)*

walk *(v)*

THEME 6
Art and Literature

architect *(n)*

architecture *(n)*

art *(n)*

biographer *(n)*

biography *(n)*

get *(v)*

give *(v)*

literature *(n)*

meet *(v)*

move *(v)*

novelist *(n)*

paint *(v)*

painter *(n)*

painting *(n)*

play *(n and v)*

playwright *(n)*

poem *(n)*

poet *(n)*

sculptor *(n)*

sculpture *(n)*

see *(v)*

send *(v)*

stop *(v)*

take *(v)*

teach *(v)*

write *(v)*

THEME 7
Sports and Leisure

ball *(n)*

beach *(n)*

cinema *(n)*

film *(n)*

football *(n)*

leisure *(n)*

mall *(n)*

music *(n)*

play *(v)*

radio *(n)*

shopping *(n)*

sport *(n)*

stadium *(n)*

surfing *(n)*

swimming *(n)*

television *(n)*

tennis *(n)*

theatre *(n)*

watch *(v)*

Word Lists: Alphabetical

THEME 8
Nutrition and Health

bread *(n)*
butter *(n)*
cheese *(n)*
chicken *(n)*
coffee *(n)*
drink *(n and v)*
eat *(v)*
egg *(n)*
fish *(n)*
food *(n)*
fruit *(n)*
ice-cream *(n)*
juice *(n)*
meat *(n)*
milk *(n)*
potato *(n)*
rice *(n)*
salad *(n)*
sandwich *(n)*
sugar *(n)*
tea *(n)*
vegetable *(n)*
water *(n)*

accountant *(n)*
adult *(n)*
afternoon *(n)*
answer *(n and v)*
architect *(n)*
architecture *(n)*
art *(n)*
ask *(v)*
baby *(n)*
ball *(n)*
bank *(n)*
beach *(n)*
begin *(v)*
bicycle *(n)*
biographer *(n)*
biography *(n)*
black *(adj)*
blue *(adj)*
boat *(n)*
bottom *(n)*
boy *(n)*
bread *(n)*
brown *(adj)*
bus *(n)*
butter *(n)*
car *(n)*
centre *(n)*

cheese *(n)*
chicken *(n)*
child *(n)*
cinema *(n)*
cloud *(n)*
coast *(n)*
coffee *(n)*
cold *(adj)*
colour *(n and v)*
come *(v)*
computer *(n)*
country *(n)*
court *(n)*
day *(n)*
doctor *(n)*
drink *(n and v)*
drive *(v)*
east *(n)*
eat *(v)*
egg *(n)*
end *(v)*
engineer *(v)*
evening *(n)*
factory *(v)*
female *(adj)*
film *(n)*
first *(adj)*

fish *(n)*
fly *(v)*
food *(n)*
football *(n)*
friend *(n)*
fruit *(n)*
get *(v)*
girl *(n)*
give *(v)*
go *(v)*
grass *(n)*
green *(adj)*
grey *(adj)*
hospital *(n)*
hot *(adj)*
hotel *(n)*
hour *(n)*
ice-cream *(n)*
island *(n)*
job *(n)*
juice (n)
lake *(n)*
last *(adj)*
lawyer *(n)*
left *(adj)*
leisure *(n)*
listen *(v)*

literature *(n)*
male *(adj)*
mall *(n)*
man *(n)*
map *(n)*
meat *(n)*
meet *(v)*
milk *(n)*
month *(n)*
morning *(n)*
motorbike *(n)*
mountain *(n)*
move *(v)*
music *(n)*
night *(n)*
north *(n)*
novelist *(n)*
now *(adv)*
office *(n)*
old *(adj)*
orange *(adj)*
paint *(v)*
painter *(n)*
painting *(n)*
people *(n)*
person *(n)*
plane *(n)*

play *(n* and *v)*
playwright *(n)*
poem *(n)*
poet *(n)*
potato *(n)*
question *(n)*
radio *(n)*
read *(v)*
receptionist *(n)*
red *(adj)*
rice *(n)*
right *(adj)*
river *(n)*
road *(n)*
sail *(v)*
salad *(n)*
sandwich *(n)*
sculptor *(n)*
sculpture *(n)*
secretary *(n)*
see *(v)*
send *(v)*
ship *(n)*
shop *(n)*
shopping *(n)*
sky *(n)*
snow *(n)*

south *(n)*
sport *(n)*
stadium *(n)*
start *(v)*
stop *(v)*
student *(n)*
sugar *(n)*
sun *(n)*
surfing *(n)*
swimming *(n)*
take *(v)*
taxi *(n)*
tea *(n)*
teach *(v)*
teenager *(n)*
television *(n)*
tennis *(n)*
test *(n* and *v)*
theatre *(n)*
time *(n)*
today *(n)*
top *(n)*
town *(n)*
train *(n)*
tree *(n)*
typist *(n)*
vegetable *(n)*

village *(n)*
walk *(v)*
want *(v)*
watch *(v)*
water *(n)*
week *(n)*
west *(n)*
white *(adj)*
woman *(n)*
work *(n* and *(v)*
write *(v)*
wrong *(adj)*
year *(n)*
yellow *(adj)*
young *(adj)*

Tapescript

Presenter: **Starter**

Lesson 1

A Listen and point.

Voice: book
desk
chair
door
classroom
teacher
student
pen
pencil
board

Presenter: **B Listen and do.**

Voice: Open your book.
Look at page 10.
Read the first sentence.
Close your book.
Look at the board.
Open your notebook.
Write your name.
Write your phone number.
Stand up.
Sit down.

Presenter: **C Listen and answer.**

Voice: What's your name?
Are you English?
Are you at school?
Are you a student?
What class are you in?
Is your teacher American?
What's the name of your book?

Presenter: **F 1 Listen and number.**

Voice: 1 answer
2 ask
3 begin
4 end
5 question
6 student
7 test

Presenter: **G Listen and tick the next word.**

Female tutor: Open your [PAUSE] book.
Look at page [PAUSE] 10.
Read the first [PAUSE] sentence.
Look at the [PAUSE] board.
Write your [PAUSE] name.

Presenter: **H Listen and tick the question.**

Female tutor: What's your name?
Are you English?
Are you at school?
Are you a student?
What class are you in?
What's the name of your book?

Presenter: **Skills Check**

Listen. Tick the words with /e/.

Voice: desk
pen
end
begin
test
question
sentence
student
English
write
listen
answer

Presenter: **Lesson 2**

E 1 Listen.

Tutor: Hello. How are you?
Esteban: I'm fine, thanks.
Tutor: Are you a student?
Esteban: Yes, I am.
Tutor: Are you English?
Esteban: No, I'm not. I'm Spanish.
Tutor: Where are you from?
Esteban: I'm from Madrid.
Tutor: What's your name?
Esteban: My name's Esteban. Esteban Cortes.

Presenter: **E 2 Listen and answer.**

[REPEAT OF EXERCISE E1]

Presenter: **E 3 Listen and ask.**

[REPEAT OF EXERCISE E1]

Presenter: **H 2 Listen and check.**

Female student: My name's Xiu Xiu Li. I'm Chinese.
I'm from Beijing.

Presenter: **Lesson 3**
A Listen and point.

Voice 1: a time
a date
a day
afternoon
a month
evening
a week
a year
morning

Voice 2: the first day of the month
the first day of the second week
the first day of the week
the first lesson of the day
the first month of the year

Voice 1: the last day of the month
the last day of the third week
the last day of the week
the last lesson of the day
the last month of the year

Presenter: **B Listen and write.**
Part 1

Voice: Lesson 2 is at 10.
Lesson 4 is at 1.
Lesson 6 is at 3.

Presenter: **Part 2**

Voice: Lesson 1 is a test.
Lessons 2 and 3 are English.

Presenter: **C Listen and answer.**

Voice 1: Is it 2006?
Is it September?
Is it Tuesday?
Is it 10 o'clock?

Voice 2: Which year is it?
Which month is it?
Which day is it?
What's the date today?
What's the time?
When's your birthday?
How old are you?

Presenter: **F 1 Listen and number.**

Voices: 1 month
2 first
3 time
4 year
5 day
6 last
7 today
8 now
9 week

Presenter: **G Which word? Listen and circle.**

Voices: 1 What time is it?
2 When is the first lesson?
3 Which month is it?
4 What's the date today?
5 I have three lessons this evening.
6 This is my first year.

Presenter: Skills Check
Listen. Tick the correct column.

Voice: is
I'm
begin
English
fifteen
find
fine
five
listen
my
night
tick
nine
right
six
time
write

Presenter: **Lesson 4**
F 1 Listen.
Conversation 1

Teacher: Good morning. How are you?

Student: I'm fine, thanks.
Teacher: Excuse me. What's the time?
Student: It's 8.
Teacher: Thank you.

Presenter: Conversation 2
Teacher: That's nice. Is it new?
Student: Yes, it is. It's a birthday present.
Teacher: Oh, is it your birthday today?
Student: Yes, it is.
Teacher: Really? Happy birthday.
Student: Thank you.
Teacher: How old are you?
Student: I'm 18.

Presenter: Conversation 3
Teacher: Do you have a birthday party in your country?
Student: Yes, we do.
Teacher: Do you have a birthday cake?
Student: No, we don't.
Teacher: What about cards ... birthday cards?
Student: Yes, we do. We have birthday cards.

Presenter: **F 2 Listen and answer.**
[REPEAT OF EXERCISE F1]

Presenter: **F 3 Listen and ask.**
[REPEAT OF EXERCISE F1]

Presenter: **I Listen. Complete the *Student* column of the table. Tick or cross.**
Student: In my country, we have birthday presents. We have birthday cards. We don't have a party. We don't have a birthday cake.

Presenter: **Theme 1 Work and Business**
Lesson 1
A Listen and point.
Part 1
Voice 1: accountant
doctor
engineer
lawyer
receptionist
secretary
teacher
typist

Presenter: **Part 2**
Voice 1: Are you a typist?
Voice 2: Where's the doctor?
Voice 1: I want to see a lawyer.
Voice 2: This is Miss Smith, your new teacher.
Voice 1: I work in an office. I'm a secretary.
Voice 2: Do you want to be an accountant?
Voice 1: I want to be a computer engineer.
Voice 2: I work at Greenhill College. I'm a receptionist.

Presenter: **Lesson 2**
A 1 Listen and number.
Voice 1: 1 school
2 office
3 court
4 hospital
5 bank

Presenter: **A 2 Listen and write letters A to E.**
Voice 2: A Where do you go to school?
B Is there a hospital near here?
C Do you work in an office?
D What time does the court start?
E When does the bank open?

Presenter: **B 1 Listen and match.**
1
Interviewer: What do you do?
Female voice: I'm a doctor.

Presenter: 2
Interviewer: And you, sir. What do you do?
Male voice: I'm a teacher. I work at Greenhill College.

Presenter: 3
Interviewer: Excuse me. What do you do?
Female voice 1: We're lawyers.
Female voice 2: Sorry, we're late for court.

Presenter: 4
Interviewer: Sir, could you tell me your job?
Male voice: I'm a secretary.

Presenter: 5
Interviewer: What do you do?
Male voice 1: We're engineers.
Interviewer: Are you computer engineers?
Male voice 2: No, we work in a factory.

Presenter: 6
Interviewer: Are you an accountant?
Male voice: Yes, I am. I work in this bank.

Presenter: 7
Interviewer: What do you two do?
Female voice 1: We're programmers.
Female voice 2: Yeah. Programmers.

Presenter: **C Listen and tick the next word.**
1
Voice: Elena Markova lives in England, but she isn't [PAUSE] English. She's [PAUSE] Russian. She's from [PAUSE] Moscow. She's [PAUSE] 26. She's a [PAUSE] doctor. She works in Greenhill [PAUSE] Hospital.
2
Voice: Pierre Auguste lives in Japan, but he isn't [PAUSE] Japanese. He's [PAUSE] French. He's from [PAUSE] Paris. He's [PAUSE] 33. He's an [PAUSE] engineer. He works in a car [PAUSE] factory.
3
Voice: Bulent Okan is [PAUSE] Turkish. He's [PAUSE] 45. He's from Ankara, but he now lives in [PAUSE] Istanbul. He's an [PAUSE] accountant. He works in a large [PAUSE] bank.
4
Voice: Paola Franchetti lives in Switzerland, but she isn't [PAUSE] Swiss. She's [PAUSE] Italian. She's a [PAUSE] lawyer. She's [PAUSE] 29. It's [PAUSE] 10.00 and she's in [PAUSE] court.

Presenter: **D Listen and complete the ID card.**
Voice: Jill Cast works at Greenhill Bank. She is British. She lives in Greenhill now, but she comes from London. She works in the computer department. She's a computer programmer. She's 23.

Presenter: **Skills Check**
Listen. Tick the correct column.
Voice: are
class
date

Presenter: **Lesson 3**
B 1 Listen. Identify the sounds.
Sound effects:
1 typewriter
2 classroom noises
3 courtroom noises
4 someone dictating a letter
5 factory noises
6 accounting machine and mumbling of numbers
7 hospital noises
8 computer noises
9 noises from the reception area of an office

Presenter: **B 2 Listen again. Who works here?**
[REPEAT OF EXERCISE B1]

Presenter: **Lesson 4**
A 1 Listen.
Receptionist: Can I help you?
Carl: I have a meeting with Mrs Dart.
Receptionist: What's your name, please?
Carl: Carl Clark.
Receptionist: How do you spell that?
Carl: C-A-R-L C-L-A-R-K.
Receptionist: Thank you, Mr Clark.
Mrs Dart? Mr Clark is here.
Mrs Dart: Thank you. Send him in.

Presenter: **A 2 Listen and ask.**
[REPEAT OF EXERCISE A1]

Presenter: **C 1 Listen.**
Mrs Dart: Good morning, Mr Clark. How are you?
Carl: I'm fine, thanks.
Mrs Dart: I'm Mrs Dart.
Carl: I'm pleased to meet you.
Mrs Dart: Come in. Sit down.
Carl: Thank you.

Mrs Dart: How old are you, Carl?
Carl: I'm 19.
Mrs Dart: Are you English?
Carl: No, I'm Canadian.

Mrs Dart: So, what do you want to do?
Carl: I want to work with computers.
Mrs Dart: Do you want to be a programmer? Or do you want to be an engineer?
Carl: A programmer, I think.
Mrs Dart: Well, the classes start on September 25th ...

Presenter: **C 2 Listen and answer.**
[REPEAT OF EXERCISE C1]

Presenter: **C 3 Listen and ask.**
[REPEAT OF EXERCISE C1]

Presenter: **E 2 Listen and check.**
Andrea: My name is Andrea Totti. I'm Italian. I'm 20. I'm at Greenhill College. I want to work with numbers. I want to be an accountant.

Presenter: **Theme 2 Science and Nature**
Lesson 1
A Listen and point.
Voice: sky
clouds
sun
trees
snow
sand
grass
mountain

The sky is blue.
The clouds are black.
The snow is cold.
What colour are the trees?
The sun is hot today.
The sand is orange.
The grass is green.

Presenter: **B Listen and find.**
Voice: Find something yellow.
Find something orange.
Find something white.
Find something black.
Find something green.
Find something brown.
Find something blue.
Find something grey.
Find something red.

Presenter: **C Listen and answer.**
Voice: What colour is the snow?
What colour is the sun?
What colour is the sky?
What colour is the sand?
What colour are the trees?
What colour are the clouds?
What colour are the mountains?

Presenter: **Lesson 2**
A 2 Listen and point.
Voice: It's cold.
It's hot.
It's very cold.
It's very, very hot.
It's very hot.
It's very, very cold.

Presenter: **B 2 Listen and check.**
1
Voice: What is it?
It is snow.
What colour is it?
It is white.

Presenter: 2

Voice: What are they?
They are clouds.
What colour are they?
They are black.

Presenter: 3

Voice: What is it?
It is grass.
What colour is it?
It is green.

Presenter: 4

Voice: What is it?
It is the sun.
What colour is it?
It is yellow.

Presenter: 5

Voice: What are they?
They are trees.
What colour are they?
They are brown.

Presenter: 6

Voice: What is it?
It is sand.
What colour is it?
It is orange.

Presenter: **C Listen and draw.**

Voice: Look at the picture.
You can see some mountains.
Draw the sun in the sky.
Draw four clouds in the sky.
One cloud is white. Two clouds are grey. One cloud is black.
Draw some snow on the mountains.
Draw some grass and some trees.

Presenter: **D Listen. Find and number six items in the picture in Lesson 1.**

Voice:
1 It is very, very, very hot. In the morning and the evening it is red. During the day it is yellow or orange. [PAUSE] It is the sun.
2 At night it is black. In the morning it is grey and then blue. [PAUSE] It's the sky.
3 Sometimes they are white, sometimes they are black, sometimes they are grey. [PAUSE] They are clouds.
4 It is sometimes yellow or orange. In some places, it is red. In other places, it is white. You find it in hot places. [PAUSE] It is sand.
5 It is usually green, but when it is very hot and very dry it is brown. [PAUSE] It is grass.
6 In cold months they are brown. In hot months they are brown and green. Sometimes they have red or yellow or blue or orange parts. [PAUSE] They are trees.

Presenter: **E Listen. What is it?**

Voice: It is in the sky when there are clouds and the sun is shining. It is red, orange, yellow, green, blue, indigo and violet. [PAUSE] It is a rainbow.

Presenter: **Skills Check 1**
Listen and check.

Voice: grass
grey
red
white
sky
yellow

Presenter: **Skills Check 2**
Listen. Tick the words with /iː/.

Voice: tree
blue
green
he
grey
see
she
we
the

Presenter: Lesson 3

B Listen. Which drawing is it?

Presenter: A

Voice: The drawing has lots of squares. They are all black. It has grey lines between the black squares. It has white circles at the corners of the squares.

Presenter: B

Voice: The drawing has four squares. Each square has another square in the middle. Two large squares are grey, one is black and one is white. All the small squares are grey.

Presenter: C

Voice: There are three circles. They are brown. The circles have a small section missing.

Presenter: D

Voice: The drawing has two main circles. There are other circles around these two main circles. The circles around one circle are small. The circles around the other circle are large.

Presenter: E

Voice: The drawing has two squares. One square has coloured squares – red, light blue, violet and yellow. One square is white. There is a black circle in the middle of each square.

Presenter: Lesson 4

A 2 Listen.

Conversation 1

Lee: Look at this drawing.

Kim: Which drawing?

Lee: This one. Number 2. What can you see?

Kim: I can see black squares.
[PAUSE]

Lee: What else can you see?

Kim: There are lines. What is this colour?

Lee: It's grey.

Kim: How do you say the word?

Lee: Grey.

Kim: Grey. OK. There are grey lines.
[PAUSE]

Lee: Anything else?

Kim: Oh, yes. I can see white circles.

Lee: How many circles are there?

Kim: There are … I can't count them! They change from white to black! I don't understand. Why do they do that?

Presenter: A 3 Listen and read.
[REPEAT OF EXERCISE A2]

Presenter: A 4 Listen and answer.
[REPEAT OF EXERCISE A2]

Presenter: C 2 Listen.

Conversation 2

Teenage boy: Look at this drawing.

Teenage girl: Which drawing?

Teenage boy: This one. Number 4. What can you see?

Teenage girl: I can see four squares.

Teenage boy: What colour are they?

Teenage girl: One square is red, one is blue, one is yellow and … what colour is that?

Teenage boy: It's violet.

Teenage girl: How do you say the word?

Teenage boy: Violet.

Teenage girl: Violet. OK. And one square is white.
[PAUSE]

Teenage boy: What else can you see?

Teenage girl: There is a black circle in the middle of the coloured squares, and there's a black circle in the middle of the white square.

Teenage boy: OK. Cover the white square.

Teenage girl: Yes.

Teenage boy: Look at the black circle in the middle of the coloured squares.

Teenage girl: OK. What next?

Teenage boy: No! Look for 30 seconds.

Teenage girl: Right.

Teenage boy: OK. Now cover the coloured squares. Look at the black circle in the middle of the white square. What can you see?

	[PAUSE]
Teenage girl:	I can see … Oh! I can see colours. I can see four coloured squares. Blue, orange, or red, yellow and … What is the name of the colour?
Teenage boy:	Violet.
Teenage girl:	That's amazing! Why does that happen?

Presenter: **Theme 3 The Physical World**

Lesson 1

A Listen and point.

Voice:
city
town
village
island
lake
mountain
river
coast
north
south
east
west
centre
northeast
southwest
northwest
southeast

There are mountains in the northwest.
There is a lake in the southeast.
There is a large island.
There is a town in the north.
There are mountains in the south.
There is a city on the coast.
There is a city on a river.
There is a village on a lake.
There is a town in the centre.

Presenter: **B Listen and find.**

Voices:
1 I live in a town. It is on the coast.
2 I live in a village. It is on two rivers.
3 I live on an island. It is a very small island. There is only one village.
4 I live in a town. It is in the south of the country. I don't live on the coast. I live in the mountains.
5 I live in a town in the east of the country. It is in the mountains.

Presenter: **Lesson 2**

A 1 Listen and number.

Voices:
1 My house is high up in the mountains.
2 I live in a small house on a lake.
3 I come from a tiny village on an island.
4 There is a small river in my town.
5 I come from the capital city of my country.

Presenter: **B 1 Listen and number.**

Man: I am from a large country called Polonia. I come from a village. Well, no, it's not a village really. It's a small town. It is in the *east*. It isn't near the coast. It's high up in the mountains. It's very cold in December and January, but it's hot in June and July.

Presenter: **C Listen and draw.**

Woman: I come from a small country called Borland. The capital city is in the centre of the country. It is called Bor – B-O-R. But I come from the west of the country. My town is on the coast. It is called Ethios – E-T-H-I-O-S. It's very hot in August, but it's quite cold in February. My town is on a river. It is the River LASK – L-A-S-K. The river comes from a lake. The lake is in the mountains in the southeast of the country. Bor, the capital, is on the River Lask, too.

Presenter: **Skills Check 1**

Listen and check.

Voice: west

river
east
island
lake
left
city
right
centre
village

Presenter: **Skills Check 2**

Listen. Tick the words with /aʊ/.

Voice: south
town
country
mountain
coast
hour
now
brown
around
snow
yellow
accountant
cloud
cold

Presenter: **Theme 4 Culture and Civilization**

Lesson 1

A Listen and point.

Voices: a man
a woman
a boy
a girl
a child
an adult
a female person
a male person
an old person
a young person

Voices: boys
girls
men
women
children
adults
females
males
friends

Voices: One man is talking.
The women are working.
There are two boys.
There are four girls.
I can see eight adults in the pictures.
There are two children in the picture.
There are nine females in the pictures.
I can see five males.

Presenter: **B Listen and find.**

Voice: Circle one person.
Circle one boy.
Circle the girls.
Circle the boys.
Circle the women.
Circle the men.
Circle the adults.
Circle the children.
Circle the people.
Circle the male people.
Circle the female people.

Presenter: **D Listen. True or false?**

Voice:
1 There are eight adults. There are five women and three men.
2 There are fourteen people. There are five male people and nine female people.
3 There are six children, four girls and two boys.
4 There aren't any female children.

Presenter: **Lesson 2**

A 1 Listen and number.

1

Voice 1: How old are you?

Girl: Thirteen.

Voice 1: Ah, so you're a teenager now.

2

Voice 2: She is a nurse. She works in a hospital. She's about 35.

3

Voice 1: What a lovely baby! How old is she?

Voice 2: She's 18 months.

4

Man: It's strange, you know. I'm 80, but I don't feel like an old person.

5

Woman 1: Do you have any children?

Woman 2: Yes, I have one child. He's 10.

Presenter: **A 2 Listen and answer.**

Voice: 1 How old is the baby?
2 How old is the boy?
3 What about the teenager?
4 Is the woman about 50?
5 Is the old person about 60?

Presenter: **B 2 Listen and check.**

Lecturer: In British culture, we use the word *baby* for the first eighteen months to two years of life. Then the baby becomes a *child*. We use the word *child* for boys and girls between the ages of two and twelve. Then we have a special word – *teenager*. The word comes from the numbers between thirteen and nineteen. They all end in *teen*. So a person who is thirteen, fourteen, fifteen, and so on, is a *teenager*. Finally, we have the word *adult*. We use the word for people from twenty up to, well, a hundred. But sometimes we say *He is old* or *He is an old man* for someone over sixty-five or seventy.

Presenter: Skills Check 1
Listen and check.

Voice: men
female
women
child
teenager
male
people
children
friend
baby

Presenter: Skills Check 2
Listen. Tick the words with /æ/.

Voice: adult
ask
last
can
can't
Saturday
male
lake
woman
man
map
village

Presenter: Lesson 3
B Listen. Which photograph is it?

Voice: 1 There are five children in the picture. They are with a woman. I think she is their teacher.
2 There are two people in the picture. There's a man and a woman. They might be brother and sister, or maybe they are married.
3 There are seven people in the picture. They are teenagers. I think they're students. They are sitting outside a building. It's probably a college.
4 There are two people in the picture. There is a woman. She is holding a baby. She is a doctor. I don't think she's the baby's mother.
5 There are a lot of old people in the picture. They look very happy. Maybe they are old friends.

6 There are five people in the picture. There are three men and two women. They are all quite old. One of the men is wearing glasses.

Presenter: **Lesson 4**

A 1 Look at the conversation and listen.

Female student: What are you doing?

Male student: I'm learning these words. We have a test on Tuesday.

Female student: Can I help you?

Male student: Yes, thanks.

[PAUSE]

Female student: What do you call this in English?

Male student: It's a baby.

[PAUSE]

Female student: How do you spell *people*?

Male student: P-E-O-P-L-E.

Female student: P-E-O-...?

Male student: P-L-E.

[PAUSE]

Female student: How do you say this word?

Male student: *'Adult.*

Female student: *A'dult?*

Male student: No, *'adult*. The stress is on the first syllable.

[PAUSE]

Female student: What does *teenager* mean?

Male student: It's a person from the age of thirteen to nineteen.

[PAUSE]

Female student: What is the plural of *woman*?

Male student: *Women.*

Female student: How do you spell that?

Male student: W-O-M-E-N.

Female student: And how do you say it?

Male student: *'Women.*

Female student: Well done.

Male student: Thanks.

Female student: Not at all.

Presenter: **D 3 Listen and check your answers.**

Voice: adult
people
woman
women
children
babies
person
culture

Presenter: **Theme 5 They Made Our World**
Lesson 1

A Listen and point.

Voices: a bicycle
a boat
a bus
a car
a plane
a ship
a train
a road
a lake
the sky
the sea
tracks

Voices: There is a boat on the lake.
There are four cars on the road.
I go to work by bus.
How many planes are there in the picture?
Where's the ship going?
Have you got a bicycle?
Are there many people on the train?
Do you like walking?

Presenter: **B Listen and complete the table.**
Part 1

Voice: How do most people get to work? According to a recent survey, most people in New Zealand go to work by car. The researchers say that one million people go to work by car each day.

Presenter: **Part 2**

Voice: Walking is in second place. ninety-three thousand people walk to work. In third place is the bus. Fifty-two thousand people go to work by bus each day. Nearly sixty thousand people ride to work. Forty-one thousand go by bicycle and seventeen thousand go by motorbike. Only fifteen thousand go by train. Thirteen thousand people go to work by another method. For example, on rollerskates or on a skateboard!

Presenter: **Part 3**

Voice: We can look at these numbers in a different way. What percentage of people go to work by car in New Zealand? The answer is eighty-one point two percent. Here are the percentages for the other methods. Walking – seven point six percent. Going by bus – four point two percent. Bicycle – three point three percent. Motorbike – one point four percent, and going by train – one point two percent. All the other methods added up to one point one percent.

Presenter: **D Listen. True or false?**

Voice: The car is the most popular method.
Walking is more popular than riding a bicycle.
The bicycle is in third place.
The train is not as popular as the bus.
Nearly sixty thousand people ride to work.
Nearly ten percent of people go by bicycle or motorbike.

Presenter: Lesson 2
A 1 Listen and number.

Voice: 1 drive
2 ride
3 walk
4 sail
5 fly

Presenter: **A 2 Listen and answer.**

Voice: Do you drive to college?
Do you have a bicycle?
Do you walk a lot?
Can you fly a plane?
Where can you sail in your country?

Presenter: **B 2 Listen and check.**

Voices: The record speed for a plane is seven thousand, six hundred and ninety-two point six six kilometres per hour. The record was set on 28th March, 2004.

The record speed for a car is one thousand, two hundred and twenty-seven point nine eight kilometres per hour. The record was set on 15th October, 1997.

The fastest speed for a motorbike is five hundred and eighteen point four five. This record was set on 14th July, 1990.

On 18th May, 1990, a train travelled at five hundred and fifteen point three zero kph.

What is the record speed for a bicycle? Fifty kph? One hundred? Two hundred? On 3rd October, 1995, a bicycle travelled at two hundred and sixty-eight point eight three kilometres per hour. The bicycle was behind a car.

Presenter: **Skills Check 2**
Listen and check.

Voice: bicycle
drive
fly
plane
sail
ship
street
train
track
motorbike

Presenter: **Skills Check 3**
Listen. Tick the words with /əʊ/.

Voice: boat
do
does
don't
go
goes
motor
home
how
know
no
now
road
phone
long

Presenter: **Lesson 3**
B Listen. What is it?

Sound effects: 1 motorbike
2 bus
3 car
4 plane
5 ship
6 train
7 boat
8 bicycle

Presenter: **C 1 Listen.**
Female student: How do you get to college?
Male student: I come by car.
Female student: How long does it take?
Male student: About forty-five minutes.
Female student: Forty-five minutes! How far is it?
Male student: It's only about ten kilometres. But the traffic is very bad.

Presenter: **C 2 Listen and answer.**
[REPEAT OF EXERCISE C1]

Presenter: **Lesson 4**
B Marc and Simone are talking about the figures. Listen.
Marc: Simone?
Simone: Yes?
Marc: How do you say this word?
Simone: Which word?
Marc: This one. T-R-A-M.
Simone: *Tram.*
Marc: *Tram.* Right. What does it mean?
Simone: A tram is a kind of bus. It goes on tracks on the road.
Marc: Oh, yes. I know. What about this one – *Under'ground.*
Simone: Oh, yes. *The 'Underground.*
Marc: Where is the stress?
Simone: It's on the first syllable.
Marc: *'Underground.*
Simone: That's right.
Marc: So what does it mean?
Simone: It's a kind of train. It goes under the ground.
Marc: Oh, right. Like the subway in New York.
Simone: Yes, and the métro in Paris.

Presenter: **Theme 6 Art and Literature**
Lesson 1
B Listen and point.

Voices: painting
sculpture
architecture
novel
play
poem
biography

Voices: Do you like the plays of William Shakespeare?
Have you read the new biography of Charles Dickens?
I love this poem. It's by Thomas Hood.
I'm very interested in architecture.
This sculpture is very famous.
What a lovely painting! Who is the painter?
Who wrote this novel?

Presenter: **C Listen to the lecture. Number the paintings.**
Part 1
Female lecturer: There are three main kinds of art in

Western culture. There is painting, sculpture and architecture. However, I'm not going to talk about sculpture or architecture today. I'm going to concentrate on painting.

Presenter: **Part 2**

Female lecturer: There are four main kinds of painting in Western culture. Firstly, there are portraits. A portrait is a painting of a person. You can usually see just the head and shoulders, but sometimes you can see the whole person. The person is usually looking out of the painting at you. Many portraits show famous people, but the most famous portrait of all shows the face of an unknown woman. It is called the *Mona Lisa*. It is by the Italian painter, Leonardo da Vinci.
The second kind of painting is the landscape. A landscape shows a piece of land – perhaps it is a mountain, or a river, or trees or a field of flowers. Sometimes there are people in a landscape painting, but they are not important. The painter is interested in the land itself. Claude Monet, the French painter, did many landscapes, including *Corn Poppies*.
The third kind of painting is the seascape. A seascape painting is similar to a landscape, but, of course, the important thing is the sea. Sometimes there are boats or ships in the picture, but sometimes we can just see the sea, calm or stormy. The English painter, Turner, did a lot of seascapes, including *The Fighting Temeraire*.
The fourth kind of painting is called a still life. In a still life painting, we can see some flowers or some fruit – apples, oranges, pears, grapes. There are some very famous still life paintings, including *Sunflowers* by the Dutch painter, Vincent Van Gogh.

Presenter: **D Listen and answer.**

Voice:
1 How many main kinds of paintings are there in Western culture?
2 Can you name one of the kinds?
3 What kind of painting is picture 1?
4 What about ppicture 2?
5 What can you see in a still life painting?
6 What kind of painting has boats or ships?

Presenter: **Lesson 2**

Introduction

Female lecturer: Every culture has its own art and literature. I'm not going to talk about art today. I'm going to talk about literature in Western culture.

Presenter: **The lecture**

Female lecturer: There are four main kinds of literature. Firstly, there are novels. A novel is a story. Novels often tell the story of a person's life, but the story is not true. The most famous novelist in English literature is Charles Dickens. One of his most famous novels is *Oliver Twist*.
The second kind of literature is the biography. A biography is also the story of a person's life, but it is the life of a real person. There are biographies of every famous person in the world.
Thirdly, there are plays. A play is also a story. Actors bring the story to life in a theatre. The most famous playwright in English literature is William Shakespeare. He wrote many plays, including *Romeo and Juliet*.
Finally, there are poems. A poem is often about one idea. Many poems

have words with similar sounds. We call this *rhyme*. For example, *say* and *play*, or *right* and *night*.

Presenter: **A 2 Listen and check.**

Female lecturer: There are special names for people who make art or literature. For example, *painter*, *sculptor*, *poet*. But we can divide people into two groups. Firstly, there are the artists. This group contains painters, like Leonardo da Vinci, and sculptors, like Michelangelo. It also contains architects, like the American, Frank Lloyd Wright. Secondly, we have the writers. This group comprises novelists like the English woman, Jane Austen, and poets, like the American woman, Emily Dickinson. It also contains playwrights. The most famous playwright in the world is, of course, William Shakespeare. Finally, this group includes biographers. A biographer writes the story of another person's life, like James Boswell who wrote the story of Dr Johnson's life.

Presenter: **B 2 Listen and check.**
[REPEAT OF EXERCISE A2]

Presenter: **C 2 Listen and check.**

Voice: writer
painter
sculptor
literature
biographer
sculpture
architecture

Presenter: **Skills Check 3**
Listen and check.

Voice: literature
seascape
writer
poet
still
life
kind
painter
art
landscape
play
architect
portrait

Presenter: **Lesson 4**
A 1 Listen.

Andy: Who is the most famous writer in your culture?
Hosni: I think it's Naguib Mahfouz.
Andy: Is that a man or a woman?
Hosni: It's a man.
Andy: How do you spell his name?
Hosni: N-A-G-U-I-B M-A-H-F-O-U-Z.
Andy: Is he alive or dead?
Hosni: He's still alive, but he's very old.
Andy: When was he born?
Hosni: I think it was about 1911.
Andy: Did he work as a writer?
Hosni: No. He worked for the Egyptian government.
Andy: What kind of literature does he write?
Hosni: Novels and short stories. He wrote three books called *The Cairo Trilogy*.
Andy: Where does he live?
Hosni: In Cairo.

Presenter: **A 2 Listen and ask.**
[REPEAT OF EXERCISE A1]

Presenter: **A 3 Listen and answer.**
[REPEAT OF EXERCISE A1]

Presenter: **B 2 Listen and check.**

Len: Who is your favourite writer?
Astrid: It's a woman called Selma Lagerlof.
Len: Who's she?
Astrid: She won the Nobel Prize for Literature in 1909.
Len: What kind of literature did she write?

Astrid: She wrote novels and short stories. She wrote a story called *The Wonderful Adventures of Nils.*

Len: What did she write about?

Astrid: She wrote about Varmland in the south of the country.

Len: Why did she write about Varmland?

Astrid: She loved the place. She was born there and she died there.

Presenter: **B 3 Listen and answer.**
[REPEAT OF EXERCISE B2]

Presenter: **B 4 Listen and ask.**
[REPEAT OF EXERCISE B2]

Presenter: **Theme 7 Sports and Leisure**
Lesson 1
B Listen and point.

Voices: playing football
going swimming
playing handball
reading a novel
watching a film
going surfing
playing tennis
going to the beach
playing chess
listening to music
going shopping

Voices: I love going swimming.
He likes playing handball.
Do you ever go surfing?
I watched a fantastic film last night.
Where can you play tennis in this town?
I'm reading a good novel at the moment.
Do you like going to the beach?
I'm not good at playing chess.
I always go shopping at the mall on Saturdays.
I like playing football, but I'm not very good at it.
My favourite leisure activity is listening to music.

Presenter: **C Listen. What am I doing?**

Sound effects:
1 an extract from a football commentary
2 surf crashing on a beach
3 the sound track of a film
4 sounds of a swimming pool
5 the noise of a Walkman as overheard
6 sounds of a tennis match
7 two people in a shop

Presenter: **D Listen and complete the table.**

Lecturer: What are the most popular leisure activities for adults in the UK? According to a recent survey, people over sixteen in the UK spend most time watching TV or films. The average time is one hundred and forty-eight minutes per day. That's almost two and a half hours each and every day.
Meeting friends is in second place. Adults spend an average of eighty-five minutes on meeting friends, that's nearly an hour and a half.
What's in third place? Playing football, perhaps, or listening to music? No, surprisingly, third place goes to reading. Yes, that's right, reading. People over sixteen in the UK spend on average nearly half an hour reading each day – twenty-eight minutes to be precise. That's all kinds of reading, novels, magazines and newspapers.
Playing sport of all kinds is in fourth place. Adults only spend about a quarter of an hour – actually fourteen minutes – on playing sport. They spend nearly as long on playing board games like chess and draughts. Thirteen minutes, to be precise. In sixth place, we have walking. Adults spend ten minutes walking each day.
Finally, we have listening to the

radio or to music on a CD. On average, adults in the UK only spend eight minutes listening to the radio or music.
These figures are for adults, for people over sixteen, in the UK. Do you think they are very different for adults in your country?

Presenter: **E Listen. True or false?**

Voice:
1 Watching TV or films is the most popular leisure activity for adults in the UK.
2 Walking is more popular than playing games.
3 Meeting friends is in third place.
4 Adults spend twice as long reading as playing sports.
5 Adults spend over five hours on leisure activities.
6 Adults spend over fifty percent of their leisure time watching TV.

Presenter: **Lesson 2**
Introduction
Part 1

Lecturer: There are many different kinds of leisure activities. One group of activities is sports. I'm not going to talk today about the other kinds of leisure activities, like reading and listening to music. I'm not even going to talk about watching sport on the television. I'm only going to talk about taking part in sports.

Presenter: **Part 2**

Lecturer: There are two main kinds of sport. Firstly, there are ball games. A ball game is simply a game played with a ball, for example, football, tennis or handball. In English, we use the verb *play* with these sports. So we say, for example, *I play football every Saturday* or *I can't play tennis* or *How do you play handball?*

The second kind of sport does not need a ball, for example, swimming or surfing. We do not use the word *play* with these sports. We say *go* instead. For example, we say *I go swimming on Sunday mornings* or *Where can you go surfing in this area?* Do you notice something about these sports? The words end in *-ing* – *swimming, surfing*.

So, how do you know which verb to use with a sport – *play* or *go*? Well, we use *play* with ball games, but we use *go* with sports which end in *-ing*. Which verb do we use with *basketball*? What about *skiing*?

Presenter: **A 1 Listen and number.**

Voice:
1 There are about ten people in this picture. They are walking. They are shopping at the mall.
2 There are thousands of people in this picture. They are sitting. They are in a very large stadium. They are watching a football match.
3 There are lots of people in this picture. They aren't standing. They are sitting. They are watching a film in a cinema.
4 There are a lot of people in this picture. They are doing step aerobics. They are at the local sports centre.
5 There are hundreds of people in this picture. They are watching a play in a theatre.

Presenter: **A 2 Listen and answer.**

Voice:
1 Is there a mall near here?
2 How often do you go to the theatre?
3 Does this place have a sports centre?
4 What is the name of the nearest football stadium?

5 What films are on at the cinema this week?

Presenter: **C Listen to the first part of a lecture.**

Part 1

Lecturer: There are two main kinds of leisure activities. The first kind is sports. I talked about sports last week. I'm not going to talk about sports activities today. I'm going to talk about the other kind of leisure activities.

Presenter: **Part 2**

Lecturer: We do some leisure activities with hundreds of other [PAUSE] people. For example, watching football in a [PAUSE] stadium, or watching a film in a [PAUSE] cinema, or watching a play in a [PAUSE] theatre. We do some leisure activities with one or two [PAUSE] friends. For example, watching television at [PAUSE] home or shopping at the [PAUSE] mall. We do some leisure activities alone, for example, reading a [PAUSE] book or listening to [PAUSE] music on a Walkman.

Presenter: **Skills Check 2**

Listen. Tick the correct column.

Voice: ball
job
watch
what
mall
orange
sport
walk
want

Presenter: **Revision**

Listen and put the words in the correct column.

Voice: beach
film
go
know
listen
play
radio
read
stadium
swim

Presenter: **Lesson 3**

C 1 Listen.

Man: How do you spend your free time?
Woman: Listening to music.
Man: Anything else?
Woman: Watching television, reading.
Man: Do you like playing sports?
Woman: No, I don't. I hate playing sports.
Man: What about watching?
Woman: Well, I like watching tennis and basketball. What about you?

Presenter: **C 2 Listen and answer.**

[REPEAT OF EXERCISE C1]

Presenter: **Lesson 4**

B Françoise and Pierre are talking about Figure 2. Listen and write each percentage in the correct place.

Françoise: What was in first place?
Pierre: Playing sport.
Françoise: What percentage of sixteen to twenty-year-olds chose that activity?
Pierre: Just under sixteen percent. Say fifteen point five percent.
Françoise: What was in second place?
Pierre: Watching films. Exactly twelve percent.
Françoise: What about shopping?
Pierre: Shopping was fourth at just over six percent . Say six point five percent.

Presenter: **Theme 8 Nutrition and Health**

Lesson 1

B Listen and point.

Voice: 1 cheese
2 butter
3 bread
4 chicken
5 coffee
6 eggs
7 ice-cream
8 milk
9 orange juice
10 potatoes
11 rice
12 cola
13 chips
14 sandwiches
15 sugar
16 tea
17 water

Voice 1: Would you like some coffee?
How about a cup of tea?
Do you take sugar?
Voice 2: I don't want milk, thank you.

Voice 1: Would you like some more potatoes or chips?

Voice 3: I had a cheese sandwich for lunch.
Voice 1: Did you? I had chicken and rice.

Voice 1: Could I have a glass of water, please?
Voice 2: Would you like a soft drink – cola?
Voice 3: Do you have any orange juice?

Voice 2: My favourite food is boiled eggs. I love them.

Voice 1: It's so hot. Do you fancy an ice-cream?

Voice 3: I'd like some bread and butter with my meal, please.

Presenter: C Listen and answer.
Voice: Do you like rice?
Do you have milk in tea or coffee?
Do you put butter on your bread?
Do you prefer tea or coffee?
Do you have eggs in the morning?
Do you want a cola?
What kind of potatoes do you like?
Do you like chips?
How many teas or coffees do you drink every day?
How much sugar do you have in your tea or coffee?
How much water do you drink every day?
What's your favourite ice-cream?

Presenter: D Listen and complete the table.
Part 1
Lecturer: Today I'm going to talk about food and drinks. Why do we eat food? Why do we drink drinks? Of course, we eat because we like food, and we drink because we like drinks. But there is another reason for eating and drinking. We eat and drink to get energy. We need energy to do work. We need energy to do leisure activities. We get energy from food and drinks. Some food gives us a lot of energy. Some food only gives us a little energy. Today I'm going to tell you the energy value in certain foods and drinks. By the way, we measure energy value in calories. For example, one potato has about two hundred and seventy calories. But one portion of rice has about two hundred and ten calories. So there is more energy in one potato than in one portion of rice.

Presenter: Part 2
Lecturer: Let's look at the energy value of some other foods. One piece of chicken has an energy value of one hundred and eighty-five calories. But did you know that one piece of bread has almost as much energy? One hundred and sixty calories.

And if you put butter on the bread, that's another seventy-five calories. Yes, that's right. One hundred and sixty for the bread plus seventy-five for the butter.

Do you like ice-cream? Well, one ice-cream has one hundred and fifty calories. A glass of milk has slightly less at one hundred and forty calories. Sorry, I meant to say one hundred and thirty calories. What about soft drinks, like cola or lemonade? Actually, they have fewer calories than a glass of milk. There are about one hundred calories in a can.

There are no calories in tea or coffee. These drinks are mostly hot water. But one spoonful of sugar is twenty calories, so if you have two spoons and some milk, perhaps your cup of coffee has sixty or seventy calories.

Presenter: Lesson 2

A 4 Listen and write.

Lecturer: In today's lecture, I'm going to look at the main sources of energy from food. As you know, we need energy to do work. But where do people around the world get the energy from? Rice? Potatoes? Chicken? Or something else?

Well, the biggest source of energy is cereals. Cereals are kinds of food, like bread, pasta and rice. We spell the word *cereals* C – yes, C not S – C-E-R-E-A-L-S. Cereals.

The second biggest source of energy is sugar. There is sugar in most food from the supermarket. We also put sugar in tea and coffee and in soft drinks, like cola.

The third biggest source of energy is potatoes. In many countries, people get most of their energy from this source.

In fourth place we have vegetables, like carrots and cabbage and tomatoes. People get energy from cooked vegetables. They also get energy from vegetable juice. By the way, there is an extra letter in the word *vegetables*. We say *vegetables*, but we spell it V-E-G-E-T-A-B-L-E-S. The fifth main source of energy is fruit – that's F-R-U-I-T. That's U I in the middle. Fruit is things like bananas, mangos, pineapples. People get energy from the fruit itself and from fruit juice like orange juice and apple juice.

Finally, in sixth place we have milk and milk products, like cheese and butter.

What about meat, like lamb and beef and chicken? There is some energy in this kind of food, but meat is not a major source of energy in the world. The same is true for fish, like salmon and shark and cod. We eat a lot of fish in the world, but we do not get a lot of energy from this source.

Presenter: **B Listen and complete Table 1.**

Lecturer: How many calories do people get every day from their food? The average daily amount is one thousand, one hundred and seventeen. People get most of this amount from cereals. The average daily amount is one thousand, one hundred and eighty-nine. One, one, eight, nine. As you know, sugar is in second place. The daily amount is two hundred and thirty two calories. Potatoes are third, at one hundred and twenty six calories. The calories from vegetables and fruit are very similar – seventy-five calories for vegetables and sixty-five for fruit. Finally, the average figure for milk is thirty calories.

Presenter: **C Listen and label Figure 1.**

Lecturer: We can look at the information about daily calories in another way. On average, people get sixty-nine percent of their calories from cereals and fourteen percent from sugar – that's fourteen, not forty. They get half that amount from potatoes – that's seven percent, and four percent each from vegetables and fruit. Milk provides only two percent of the daily consumption.

Presenter: **Skills Check 2**
Listen. Tick the correct column.

Voice: fruit
blue
book
cook
could
do
juice
look
new
sugar
would

Presenter: **Lesson 3**
B 2 Listen and check.
Conversation 1

Voice 1: Would you like a sandwich?
Voice 2: Oh, yes, please.
Voice 1: What kind would you like?
Voice 2: Egg, please.

Presenter: **Conversation 2**

Voice 1: Would you like something to drink?
Voice 2: Yes, please.
Voice 1: Coffee, tea or a cold drink?
Voice 2: Tea, please.
Voice 1: How do you like it?
Voice 2: Milk and one sugar, please.

Presenter: **Conversation 3**

Voice 1: Would you like chicken or fish?
Voice 2: Could I have the fish, please?
Voice 1: Certainly. Would you like rice or potatoes with that?
Voice 2: Potatoes, please.

Presenter: **B 3 Listen and answer.**
[REPEAT OF EXERCISE B2]

Published by
Garnet Publishing Ltd.
8 Southern Court
South Street
Reading RG1 4QS, UK

This edition first published 2005
Printed with corrections 2006
Reprinted 2009

ISBN 978 1 85964 803 2

British Library Cataloguing-in-Publication Data
A catalogue record for this book is available from the British Library.

Production

Project managers:	Richard Peacock, Francesca Pinagli
Editorial team:	Rod Webb, Maggie MacIntyre
Art director:	David Rose
Design:	Mark Slader, Mike Hinks
Illustration:	Doug Nash, Karen Rose Beehive Illustration: (Colin Brown / Janos Jantner / Martin Sanders / Laszlo Veres)
Photography:	Banana Stock, Corbis, Digital Vision, flat Earth, Image Source, Ingram Publishing, Photodisc, Stockbyte

Garnet Publishing wishes to thank the following for their assistance in the piloting of this project:
David Anderson, Kaye Anderson, Alec Benson, Terry Boucher, William Davis, Jeanette Drissi, Patrick Flavin, Bruce Gunn, Marion King, Leslie Kirkham, Nicholas Lake, Mairead Lyons-Hackett, Peter Newbery, Barbara Mary Rowell, Roland Steinwand, Evan Sullivan, Yusuf Suluh, Kevin Watson, Debra Wedl, John Wells and teachers and administrators from the Higher Colleges of Technology in the UAE, and Maxine Gillway, Deborah Smock and the Fundamentals team at UGRU, UAE University.

Special thanks go to Nicola Marsden and Hinemoa Xhori.

Audio production: Chris Dalby, YellowPark

Printed and bound
in Lebanon by International Press.